THE

MESSENGER

ALSO BY JOSEPH F. GIRZONE

Jesus: His Life and Teachings

Joey

Joshua and the City

Joshua: The Gift Edition

Joshua: The Homecoming

Never Alone: A Personal Way to God

The Parables of Joshua

A Portrait of Jesus

What Is God?

THE

MESSENGER

Joseph F. Girzone

IMAGE

DOUBLEDAY

New York   London   Toronto   Sydney   Auckland

AN IMAGE BOOK
PUBLISHED BY DOUBLEDAY
a division of Random House, Inc.
1540 Broadway, New York, New York 10036

IMAGE, DOUBLEDAY, and the portrayal of a deer
drinking from a stream are trademarks of Doubleday,
a division of Random House, Inc.

Book design by Caroline Cunningham

Library of Congress Cataloging-in-Publication Data

Girzone, Joseph F.
The messenger / by Joseph F. Girzone.
p. cm.
I. Title.
PS3557.I77 M47 2002
813'.54—dc21

2001047252

ISBN 0-385-49514-5

PRINTED IN THE UNITED STATES OF AMERICA

May 2002
First Edition
1   3   5   7   9   10   8   6   4   2

Dedicated to all those good shepherds who give

untiringly of themselves to not only preach the message of

the gentle King but demonstrate its beauty in their

lives of love and compassion.

There is a wise and gentle King who has reigned for endless time over a kingdom, known as The Kingdom of Light and Peace. The kingdom rings with joyful sounds of music and laughter. It is hard for us here on earth to imagine a kingdom where everyone is happy and where there are no wars or angry outbursts to destroy the peace. Yet this kingdom is real and has existed for longer than the human mind can conceive. It is also not very far away, though it is impossible to cross from here to there, because of an impenetrable barrier as thin as a gossamer veil which guards its borders. One day the King looked down upon our world and felt a profound pity over the deplorable conditions he witnessed. He saw anger and meanness and wars and sickness and discouragement. He saw a world full of unforgivingness and intolerance. He saw good things, and good people, too, but was pained by the misery he witnessed.

After much thought and consultation with his Father, he made a momentous decision. He decided to pay a visit to this world and tell the people about himself and his Kingdom of Light, where all his subjects live in perfect joy. He would extend to them an invitation to come and live with him when their life in this world ended. So, one quiet night, when all the world was still, the King appeared, not in splendor, not in luxury as one would expect of a king, but as a little baby, born to a poor couple. As a child he became a homeless refugee, as his parents were forced to flee the insane jealousy of a demented king. As he grew from childhood to manhood, he lived like all the other villagers, so no one knew his true identity. During the last three years he spent here, he walked from village to village telling people simple stories, stories with profound truths, always pointing the way to peace and happiness, and promising that if they accepted him and his way of life they could one day come and live with him forever in his Kingdom of Light and Peace. Before he left to return home, he established a kingdom on earth as a preparation for things to come. This kingdom began with a small community of followers, with twelve men whom he appointed as leaders. To them he gave authority to spread his message throughout the world, promising to be with them until the end of time. These leaders brought the message to all the known world at the time. Wherever they went, they chose others to continue their work for the King and appointed them to take their place when they passed on. In time, some of these faithful leaders and their disciples decided to write down memories of the King and the things he taught, but not everything, because, as one of them said, "Not even the whole world could contain all the things he said and did." These writings were preserved in a sacred book which was treasured among those loyal to him. Many years later, the leaders at that time declared those writings to be an inspired way of knowing about the King's life and his message. But that was never a substitute for the authority of the leaders the King had appointed. It was still the leaders to whom the King had entrusted the responsibility to teach his message, and guaranteed to provide an ever-deepening understanding of the King's message until the end of time. As time passed, the community of followers grew to vast numbers and included people of every race and nation, as the King had planned. It became powerful and wealthy and its influence spread as its presence transcended the boundaries of all the worldly kingdoms. The King's message flourished not only in words and messages, but by the way his leaders and followers inspired changes in society. They started hospitals to care for the sick, and schools to teach the poor and the ignorant, and great universities to train scholars in the sciences and philosophy and in the understanding of all the messages contained in The Book.

In time, however, people began to center life around the kingdom. Though it was still the kingdom of the humble King, and its leaders preached his name, the memory of his goodness faded until eventually few even knew him. Oh, people liked to read The Book, in which were stories about

the King and his message, but even The Book in time became the focus of worship rather than a mirror reflecting the
King. These people broke away from the kingdom and fash-
ioned leaders of their own choosing, rejecting the leaders the
King had chosen and all the guidance of the King's spirit
through the centuries. One by one these groups splintered
into a thousand variations on the King's message, spreading
confusion throughout the kingdom. In the meantime, the
leaders of the kingdom became enamored of their power
and prestige, wearing robes common to nobility of over a
thousand years past to dramatize the importance of their
positions in the kingdom, while at the same time showing
reluctance and incapacity to change even in matters of importance to people's lives. Though many of the leaders were
good people and sensitive to the needs of the King's followers, many others felt threatened by the people's freedom and
ruled them harshly, demanding obedience to their decrees
which they often issued regardless of the pain they caused
the people. They enjoyed their power and enjoyed ruling like
rulers in other kingdoms, even though the King had forbidden this. In time, freedom was curtailed and the people were
allowed to do and think only what the leaders approved. If
they disobeyed, they were punished, often severely. Even mi-
nor leaders were reduced to a comfortable form of servitude
and lived in fear as authority became more centralized, and
everyone was monitored.

The people grew sad and restless, and were filled with
guilt because they could not live up to the demands of the

leaders. Gradually, the whole kingdom became obsessed with the endless stream of laws and penalties which the people, with the best of effort, found extremely difficult to observe. Out of discouragement they forgot the King and his message of freedom and peace. It no longer seemed real. As leaders became more concerned with the business of the kingdom, the kingdom itself became their message to the people, rather than stories about the King. Maintaining the kingdom became an obsession. The people's energy went into building up the kingdom and paying the vast debts incurred by the leaders. Thought of the King and his beautiful dream of peace and freedom faded farther and farther from view, as the people sank deeper into despair.

The King watched from afar and grew sad over what he saw happening to his dream, and wondered what he could do to reawaken hope in people's hearts. He thought and thought for the longest time, and finally decided upon a plan. One day, while walking through his splendid garden filled with flowers and plants of incredible beauty, far more beautiful than anything in the faraway kingdom, the King was reviewing all he had done to renew his faraway kingdom. He had sent messengers to reawaken people's faith. Some of those he sent were simple people who lived the King's message in the very simplicity of their lives. Ordinary people loved them, but they were often looked upon as simple, as unrealistic dreamers out of touch with reality. Memory of these holy people inspired millions of people for centuries to come. But little heed or credence was paid to them by the leaders who passed them off as harmless visionaries. The King sent other messengers who were learned to offer a new vision that would appeal to leaders, hoping they would see how far they had strayed from the humble King's dream. These messengers were often a threat because they were so brilliant. Many of them were punished, some expelled from the kingdom, and their writings banned. In time, however, many of their ideas were accepted and significant changes were made. But people's hearts did not change for long, as they soon returned to the old ways. At one point teachers appeared in the kingdom who were very angry. They, too, delivered messages but the anger behind their message was so violent it tore apart the kingdom and bred hatred and wars that continued for centuries. This broke the heart of the King, who had prayed before he returned home that his followers would always be one.

Many years passed and the kingdom showed little evidence of change. In a worldly way it was still powerful and influential but that was not what the humble King had envisioned. There were in the kingdom many people, who in their own hearts and personal lives brought joy and hope to the King. There were also many leaders who lived lives pleasing to the King, but sadly there were many who ruled the people arrogantly, imposing laws that made little sense, much like the Pharisees of old. As people became better and better educated they resented the lack of humility on the part of the leaders, and resented their condescending attitude.

Their laws and prohibitions they found offensive and foreign to the spirit of freedom and compassion of the King. The King was beside himself trying to understand what more he could do that had not already been done.

"What shall I do?" He asked himself. "I have tried everything. I have sent messengers of every description to rekindle my spirit in the kingdom, but their message is like seed on rocky soil, or barren soil where only thorn bushes will grow. It rarely takes root, and when it does it is soon dispelled by people's love of the kingdom itself which they try endlessly to protect. My messengers they judge disloyal and consider enemies because they criticize insensitive leaders. They do not understand that the kingdom must be renewed constantly so it can remain faithful to my spirit. Unfortunately, they worship the kingdom, and The Book, and care little to understand me or my wishes. I suppose it is easy to fall in love with the Kingdom. It is so majestic, and fills people with a sense of pride. I can also understand why people would die for the Kingdom, but I wonder how many would be willing to die for me, as did the saints of old, for there are not too many who even know me anymore."

The King thought long and hard. It seemed like an impossible situation. How could he guide this faraway kingdom so it would again become faithful to his spirit? How could he reacquaint his people with his life, his compassion, and his love for them. After many hours of pondering, the King finally hit upon a plan. He would send another messenger, whom he would guide in a special way.

CHAPTER

2

Meanwhile, in the faraway kingdom, there lived a simple man named Francis. As a young boy he fell in love with the King and wanted to spend his life helping others to know and love the King. He was a dreamer, and when he grew up and became a priest he found himself frequently in trouble with officials of the kingdom, who held him in very low esteem, because he did things differently. In difficult and lonely times he would take long walks, and in the quiet of his thoughts, the King would share with him his own sadness over the condition of the kingdom, which had drifted so far from his dreams. Francis did not realize that the King was trying to tell him something. At first he thought they were just his own ramblings. It took years before he realized the King was sharing something important and intimate. The realization came gradually, then as a striking awareness.

Worn down by the stress of his work, and in a weakened state, one dark night the call of the King was unmistakable. Frightened, Francis knew his life was about to change. His doctor's call was the catalyst that brought about that change. Told he could no longer continue his work, he retired. Some colleagues sneered at the decision, attributing it to motives far from noble. Though his family was kind to him, none were aware that he was penniless. Weakened by the years of stress, he spent hours each day resting. Two years passed before he regained his strength. During that time, Francis recorded his thoughts and dreams. It was becoming increasingly clear that his sickness was not an accident. He knew he was being irresistibly drawn to something that was frightening.

It was not that he heard voices, though there were messages, messages that came in the form of ever more insistent promptings: "Do not be afraid, Francis, to follow where you are being led. Though you are weak, that is of little concern. I communicate best with those who are weak. You have been prepared for this day. Your mission means much to me, and I will be with you. I know you and I know that when the work becomes difficult you will not give up. It will be lonely, because those who should be your friends and support will be afraid or ashamed to acknowledge you. Trust no one!

"The kingdom that I love has fallen into conflict and despair. Leaders have drifted far from my message. They have fallen in love with the kingdom and have lost my spirit. Pharisees of old have sprung up again, and rule my people with the harshness of their laws and ancient customs with little concern for the people's anguish. Good shepherds are ridiculed and treated as disloyal in the same way I was treated by the masters of the old law. Fearful, they rarely speak out. Indeed, they are forbidden to speak out. It is considered offensive and insubordinate.

"So, I am sending you to speak out, and to speak out forcefully to lift the spirits of the people and rouse their courage and assure them I have not forgotten them. Encoded in your heart are all the messages I have been giving you over the years. Now speak them out loudly and clearly. Do not prepare what you are to say because those to whom you speak will be always different. You will know what to say when the time comes. Your very presence will deliver the most powerful message, the message of my spirit touching the hearts of the good and arousing the anger of those who worship the kingdom, but do not know me. They will judge you an enemy and try to destroy and discredit you. But do not be afraid. I am determined your mission will succeed, though you will not see it in your time. Do not stay in one place, but move from place to place. When you are finished you will return to me."

Francis was thrilled that, in spite of his weakness, he still had a purpose, a mission. He knew it was the King prompting him, and he knew he could fulfill the King's wishes, but it was not a task he would have chosen on his own. It would be a difficult task. Early on in his priesthood experience had taught him to depend on himself and his own resources, as others could not be trusted in critical times. But he had no idea that the difficulties before him would be so overwhelming. Loneliness he had known. This was something other than that. It was isolating him and making him alone in his Father's house, and even among his friends. He would always be viewed with suspicion.

The nights that followed were spent sleeping fitfully, dreaming of the King's faraway kingdom as if it were not all around him, but far out in space. He saw it as a tiny light on a planet faraway. Though this little light was like many other lights in the heavens, he knew it was different, because, among all the millions of lights in the universe, this was the jewel of the King's creation. That is why the King was sad— because this precious kingdom had drifted so far from its ideal and from the memory of his presence long ago.

Francis could see himself moving through space as he approached the faraway kingdom. From a distance it appeared like a tiny light, bright and colorful, a happy place. He soon saw that it was not. Signs of hostility and pain were everywhere. He suddenly felt the King's sadness. It made him realize what his mission would have to be.

Days passed rapidly as Francis put his affairs in order. He wondered when his work would begin. A call of some sort would come he knew, but when, and how, and where? He knew he had always been popular. The people liked what he preached. His messages brought peace and healing, and, more importantly, a sense of the King's presence.

That first call did come and it was a phone call, an invitation to a quiet part of the country. Francis was happy to accept it.

• • •

When he arrived, the bishop refused to see him or to even welcome him. It was a painful rejection. He had been prepared for as much, but when it finally happened it hurt. Francis stayed that night at a local inn.

The following day he delivered his message. "The King is offended because his people have forgotten him. He realizes he is rarely spoken of in the kingdom. Few even know him anymore. It seems the King's humility is an embarrassment to officials who glory in their princely office, and treat their priests like servants, depriving them of their God-given human rights. Their messages rarely reflect the King's spirit of freedom and joy that he wanted for his people. They may call him, 'Lord,' but their hearts are far from him. They sing his name, but it is so often only an empty sound. It seems the whole world has become enamored of the kingdom and has forgotten the King. I come to you as a simple messenger to remind you of the King, and how he loves you. Do not lose hope in him. He did not intend that your lives be governed so harshly. He came to welcome and heal, but his spirit of gentle shepherding has been replaced by many overbearing shepherds who craft laws that have kept you at a distance from the King and make you feel unworthy to sit at his table. The King feels sad that you have been taught to fear him and his Father.

" 'Do not be afraid,' he says to you. 'I love you with an endless and unconditional love. I understand your goodness and your weaknesses. I see and feel your pain. I am ever by your side and, indeed, in your heart, especially when you need me. But know beyond all else that I love you.' "

The people received Francis' message with joy. The bishop attended the talk, as well as his whole staff. After the talk, however, he walked out without speaking to anyone. When Francis asked to talk to him, he refused. One of the bishops, with tears in his eyes, embraced Francis and told him to have courage and not give up. Two days after the talk, the chancellor asked the bishop what he thought of the talk. "I agreed with everything he said, everything, but I am too old to fight for any more change. I am just glad everyone had a chance to hear him."

Word, however, was spread to other bishops that Francis had a bad attitude toward the kingdom, and could do damage. Other bishops received reports of the talk and knew what Francis had really said and they were happy. Those in love with their lofty positions in the kingdom were saddened and angry. Good shepherds, however, were delighted at what he said.

CHAPTER

3

The next place to which Francis was called was the territory of a friendly archbishop. He was a brilliant man, perhaps the brightest of all the bishops. He had suffered much because of his openness and his concern for the bruised and hurting sheep in the kingdom. Because of his care for the people and his courage in speaking out, petty Vatican officials made sure he was deprived of honors offered to him by prestigious universities. But being a soul of greater stature than those who persecuted him, he was little offended by the slight.

When Francis arrived there, he was warmly greeted and treated with dignity, a comfort he did not expect. The archbishop welcomed him warmly, and allowed a biblical scholar of great renown, who valued Francis' writings, to introduce him to the people. The setting was a banquet to which people from far and wide were invited, people of The Book, as well as people of Tradition. The talk was scheduled for the following day. It showed everyone present how simple and easy unity could be when Jesus was the focus.

"My friends," he began, "I am grateful to your bishop for his kindness and warm welcome. I know he is a blessing to all of you. I want you all to know that a new day is not far off. Your community here must be a comfort to the King because his spirit is alive and thriving here. But it is not the same in so many other places. Even the very human rights of priests are denied, and bishops, rather than being respected as successors of the apostles, are treated as servants of Vatican secretaries, and are punished when they speak out and act with courage.

"The King is rarely spoken of, and his spirit never considered when decisions are made in high places. The King is deeply troubled over what has become of his kingdom for which he had such great hopes. He knows that many of you, in your discouragement over life throughout the kingdom, may have drifted from one place to another, trying to find love and acceptance. This fragmenting of the kingdom is not good. This in itself pains the King who wanted so much for his followers to always be one as a powerful evidence of the divine origin of his kingdom. But now, even though we have become fragmented, we must reach out to one another and find our way to wholeness once more. You have come here today because you share one thing in common. You love the

King and are eager to learn more about him. I realize his
memory has faded from many hearts, and in some places has
been all but lost. But, today is a new day. The King wants you
to know that you are on his mind continually. He loves you
with a boundless love, and is concerned about your pain and
anguish. He knows many of you are troubled because you
feel you have failed in your commitment as loyal citizens of
the kingdom, and feel unworthy that you cannot measure up
to all the requirements of the law. He wants you to know that
he once freed you from the law, and the only law in the kingdom that binds you now is the law to love his Father and love
one another as you love yourselves. All other requirements
are to be evaluated judiciously according to the King's spirit.
It is his people he cares about, not the laws. So do not feel
you have failed, when, through weakness you have stumbled
along the way. He knows that life here in this world is not
easy and is often so complicated that it is difficult to make
personal decisions with any assurance that they are the right
decisions. To be punished by religious authorities for those
decisions adds to your discouragement. That is because they
do not have the mind of the Good Shepherd who could understand your problems. He wants you to know that he understands. As long as you are sincere in following him, and in
caring for one another, he overlooks your many failings as he
overlooked the failings of the woman in Simon the Pharisee's
house so many years ago, and of the poor sinner begging for
forgiveness in the back of the temple.

"I see that all of you here today represent many divisions

of the kingdom. Today, however, you are one. Would not the King be pleased if we were to draw even closer to one another until we realize that we are one family in his Father's love. Work tirelessly toward that goal. In doing this you will again make real the King's presence not only in the kingdom, but throughout the world. Do not be intimidated by those in love with 'the traditions of the ancients.' They would preserve the divisions for fear of diluting their beliefs. They will one day understand that the King values love and compassion over the rigidness of law. His spirit must again break through the letter of the law which crushes the spirit.

"What you have is a good spirit that must spread. May the Holy Spirit continue to guide you and bless your efforts as you reach out to one another."

•   •   •

The people applauded Francis' message enthusiastically. It was what they needed to hear. It was not only a comfort to them, but gave validity to the work of their bishop who had struggled hard to breathe life into his part of the kingdom.

CHAPTER

4

When Francis left that city he returned home. Plane trips and talks were strenuous and demanding. Resting at home and working in the garden was not only a pastime; it was a necessity. Living alone provided the solitude to wander through the woods, and think, and sense a presence that gave him life. Even though he was alone he never felt alone. There was a presence nearby. It was this presence, never talking, always quiet, reassuring, that, in spite of adverse experiences, everything was unfolding as planned. It was like a soothing balm—healing, energizing, giving strength for whatever might lie ahead.

One of the insights which were becoming stronger was the ever increasing divisions of the kingdom, as men sprung up like mushrooms, starting their own communities, preaching their own gospel, further dividing and weakening the kingdom. The King had arranged for orderly transmission of authority to teach within the kingdom. These people worked outside that authority, becoming an authority unto themselves. The problem was that this was becoming acceptable among people of The Book. Anyone could start his or her own religion. Originally, only God through Moses told people how he wanted to be worshipped. Then, through his Son, he established a new way with provision for passing on the new faith. It should be unthinkable that anyone dare to start another way to God, but that is what has happened since, and each day the kingdom is further splintered as men set themselves up as authorities to teach and administer, as innocent, hurting people fall prey to them. They feel that, just because they have a book, they can embark on their own ministry and teach. But the King never gave anybody a book. Authority does not come from The Book.

Authority comes down from Jesus through the Apostles. The Book has authority only because the Apostles and their successors wrote it. It merely shares in *their* authority to teach and administer the kingdom. Its acceptance as inspired is again based on their authority, as someone with authority had to proclaim it to be inspired if people had an obligation to accept it as such.

Those who go off on their own, eventually wander aimlessly and lose their way. Like branches cut off from the vine, they wither and die from lack of sustenance. Many drift away from the kingdom altogether, and become like pilgrims who enter a jungle without a compass.

It was becoming clear that Francis' mission was to reacquaint people with the King and make them aware of what was important to the King. Part of that mission was to heal, and make the King's prayer that there be "One flock and one shepherd" become a reality. This could happen only when kind shepherds welcome wandering sheep back home and treat them with tenderness rather than harshly impose the law on them.

That is why it is important for bishops to be one in Jesus' spirit. It is critical that they insist that their priests treat people with courtesy and compassion, and not demand more than fragile people can give. "It is mercy and compassion" the King demands, not more sacrifice and pain.

Those walks in the woods were for Francis precious times, as necessary to him as food and sleep. It was in those moments that his spirit was nourished and refreshed.

Occasionally, his friends Richard and Elizabeth and their sons, John and Peter, would come to visit him, or he would visit them. They had been friends for many years. Richard was his lawyer. They all took turns cooking, and shared many happy hours together. Francis could share with them things he could share with no one else. What weighed heaviest upon his heart was the pain he saw in so many people he met along the way, people who had been the victims of harsh rules, often arbitrary, and arbitrarily imposed without compassion.

Richard and Elizabeth, and even their children, had gone through much with the same kind of insensitive shepherds and teachers, but nothing could shake their loyalty to the kingdom, so Francis felt comfortable in their friendship.

During supper, which they ate on the deck overlooking their pool, the conversation drifted to Francis' latest wanderings. "Tell us, what have you been up to since we last saw you?" Richard blurted out.

"Just traveling around," Francis replied off-handedly.

"You never just travel around," Richard responded with a chuckle. "Tell us what you have really been doing."

"Really, just wandering around talking to people. I meet the nicest people sometimes. In Florida I met a man who had grown up in the North Carolina hills. He and his three brothers lived all by themselves as little children. The oldest was twelve. The youngest was four. Their father was an alcoholic and was never home. The mother had died when the children were small, so they had no one to care for them. Jack, my friend, was telling me they lived in a little house with no insulation, of course, and only a potbelly stove for heat. I asked how they kept warm. He said, 'We loaded the stove with wood, then we all piled under a big blanket on the floor near the stove and put the dog in the middle, because he was always warm. When the fire went out, our warm bodies kept each other warm.'

"When I asked if they ever went to school, he told me he never missed a day. He knew it would eventually be his ticket out of there. And it turned out to be just that. Later on, he entered the army and went to school where he earned a degree in civil planning, and then married a beautiful woman and settled down.

"While visiting Jack and his wife, Nancy, on one occasion, they were having a meeting with friends and were discussing

The Book. Most of the people were complaining about one thing or another, and how the priest had a poor singing voice and did not give good sermons. I noticed Jack kept silent.

"I asked him how he felt about all the complaints people were expressing. He said 'What they complain about doesn't bother me at all. It is such a luxury for me to just sit in the church and know that God is there in a special way for me to talk to him, I couldn't care less about the priest's faults or shortcomings. That's his problem.'

"I thought that was so beautiful. We can become so focused on incidentals that we often fail to see precious gifts lying right before our eyes.

"On another occasion I was invited to a university, a place famous for its dedication to The Book. I spoke about the King for two hours. After the talk, their theologians and scripture experts approached me and, with tears in their eyes, thanked me for speaking about the King. I was shocked because I thought that as experts in The Book, they would be familiar with the King. They proceeded to tell me 'We may have the reputation for being experts in The Book, but you have given us a flesh and blood Jesus who has lifted burdens and healed wounds we have carried all our lives. We now wonder how we could have overlooked him all these years. Thank you.' I have to admit, I was deeply affected by their humility. I never thought I would have touched people of The Book, especially since they ordinarily do not think kindly of priests. But, what I said in the beginning is true. All I do is just travel around and talk to people."

As the sun set and the night grew dark, mosquitoes invaded the deck. The first line of attack was always Francis. Whether they were of set purpose out to torture him or just liked his blood type, he was always their choice target. Unable to put up with them for very long he retreated indoors as the others followed.

"That was a great supper," Francis said. "You would never find cooking like that in a restaurant."

Elizabeth turned to look at his expression, to see if he meant it or was being facetious. Seeing his impish smile, she decided not to thank him.

"The whole evening was fun," Francis said. "It was just what I needed. Tomorrow will be a long day with an early flight to California."

Richard accompanied him to the door as he left.

CHAPTER

5

The flight was delayed due to fog, which made Francis miss his connecting flight. The next flight, cross-country to California, was pleasant enough, if one could call a long air flight pleasant. Uneventful is probably a better word. He decided not to eat on the plane, as his hosts would most probably have a reception with a few members of the planning committee and a hot supper. However, it did not turn out that way. It was supper time all right when he arrived, but all the priests were leaving the house for an engagement of some sort, and had given the cook the night off. They showed Francis his room and told him they would be back around midnight. If he wasn't so hungry he would have gone directly to bed, but instead he scouted the neighborhood for a place to eat. He eventually found a bar that served hamburgers and chicken wings.

"What'll it be, Bud?" the bartender asked.

"A dozen chicken wings and a glass of draft ale," Francis replied, then proceeded to read the newspaper he'd picked up as he left the house.

"Where'ya from?" the bartender asked as he placed the platter of hot wings and beer in front of him.

"The East Coast," Francis replied. He was not in a particularly talkative mood.

"Whereabouts?"

"Virginia, Alexandria."

"Our family used to live in Baltimore before we moved here. Really miss my friends there. Haven't seen them in years. Went back a couple of times but things have changed. Didn't recognize a soul. Didn't even recognize the old places. The friends have all moved or died off. When I asked if they knew so-and-so, I got a strange look as if I had come from outer space. It gave me a weird feeling. After a few days I came home and felt depressed all the way back. It was like I was on a different planet."

"I can imagine how you felt," Francis replied trying to be sociable while he munched on his chicken wings. "I get those kinds of looks from people, too."

The fellow went back to tending bar.

Francis left, leaving a good tip for the bartender who was grateful. "Come in anytime, fella'. It was nice meetin' ya."

Francis got back to the house just in time for his escort to pick him up for his talk. She was a kindly, middle-aged woman with whom he had originally made the speaking arrangements. Pat was her name. She apologized for the rudeness of his hosts. She felt ashamed that they did not even have the courtesy to arrange for his supper.

"That's all right," Francis said, assuring her that he was used to it. "Not too many of my colleagues are noted for their social grace," he told her. He took part of the blame for hiding the fact that he was well-known. "If they had known that, they would have treated me differently. But I prefer to be treated like anyone else, so that's what happens," Francis said with a chuckle. "It's good for my humility."

"But it is still not right. After all, you traveled four thousand miles just to talk at their place. The least they could do was give you supper."

When they arrived at the parking lot, a large crowd had already gathered. The auditorium was nearly full. People who recognized him were friendly. They had heard so much about him and had read most of what he had written. When introduced, Francis received a warm welcome.

"My dear friends," he began, "I would have traveled twice as far to be here with you this evening. A friend told me that you are a very special people, that you produce most of the food that we eat on the East Coast, so if I look too well fed, you are partly to blame.

"I have come to return the favor and bring you food. I will tell you about the King. You have a reputation in this part of the country for being loyal and dedicated to the kingdom on earth and follow meticulously its laws. For this you are to be commended. The kingdom is the pearl of great price which the King has left us as a precious heritage.

"I saw people outside picketing the talk this evening, protesting that I was not loyal to the kingdom and that I undermine the kingdom. How could one who dedicates his whole life to helping people understand the King be undermining his kingdom? Perhaps, in their excessive zeal for the kingdom they have not considered that the King himself might be disappointed with the way many things are done in the kingdom. The human element in the kingdom must constantly be renewed. The King was meek and humble and wanted his followers to follow him in his humility. Not too many have done that. Those who work hard to perfect the kingdom should be commended, and there are many among you. Those who do nothing to make the kingdom a more perfect reflection of the King are the ones who do a disservice.

"Dedication to the kingdom and observing scrupulously its laws are one thing. Understanding the King and what is important to him is critical. Unless this is a priority, love of the King cannot grow in your hearts, nor can your own spirituality grow. That pains the King deeply. The teachers of old were that way. They loved their laws and their customs, but they had little feeling for the God they professed to worship. And their meanness to his Son was despicable. History repeats itself.

"I have come to share with you this evening an understanding of the King so you can refocus your hearts upon him who has given you the kingdom. I know many of you have become followers of The Book. But remember, the King did not give you a book. The King gave you teachers whom he au-

thorized to bring his message to the whole world. If they
wrote down some of their teachings, those writings have only
as much authority as the teachers who wrote it. You cannot
take The Book and walk away from the teachers and think
you are being loyal to the King. It is true—many of the bishops and priests may not have been kind or good people, and
some may love the kingdom more than the King, but that in
no way voids the authority the King gave them. 'Do what the
scribes and Pharisees tell you, because they occupy the chair
of Moses, but do not imitate them, because they are hyp-
ocrites,' Jesus said of the teachers of old. They still deserve
our allegiance and respect, and we cannot walk away from
them without turning our backs on the King.

"Yet as serious as that is, and it is the greatest problem in
the kingdom, what troubles the King most deeply is the pain
of people who cannot measure up to the laws of the kingdom
and are treated harshly by the clergy and are cut off from the
sacraments. They are treated as unworthy of the King and
are told they are not worthy to approach him. Even worse,
many bishops do nothing about it. Jesus confronted the same
problem with the Pharisees who drove people away. That is
why he called himself the Good Shepherd, because he went
out in search of all the bruised and hurting sheep driven
away by the Pharisees, and tenderly brought them back
home. If Jesus himself chose to welcome sinners and treat
them with such tenderness, who are we to say anyone is unworthy of him. And do you think that, after bringing them
back home, he would say to them, 'All right, you stay here in
the corner, while the rest of the family has supper?'

"No matter how the clergy may treat these frail people, you yourselves must show them love and acceptance, and make them feel welcome in your midst. They have already been deeply hurt, and treated unjustly.

"There was a mother who had two children. The one never did anything wrong, and desired more than anything to see himself as perfect. But he did not love his mother, which broke her heart. The other was weak and fell many times, but each time came back to his mother brokenhearted because he hurt his mother. Will the mother treat that child harshly because of his failings? Would she not treat him tenderly, and help him in time to grow strong? That is the way it must be with those who are weak, and have difficult problems in their lives. That is the way the Good Shepherd treated the troubled and the bruised sheep. If we would be pleasing to him, we must follow his example."

• • •

Francis' talk was well-received, though there were some who were offended, because they see the kingdom as beyond criticism and anyone who criticizes the kingdom to be a traitor. When he left the hall, people with signs were still walking up and down the street. As he approached, they called him "Traitor," "Disloyal" and other names. Francis was becoming used to it. He knew they had never heard him speak or read anything he had written. They were just mindlessly reflecting the misplaced loyalty of those who loved the kingdom right or wrong, and had just heard rumors about Francis. Even though they never met him, they made no effort to become acquainted with him. Francis knew that if the King himself came back in disguise and exposed abuses even more forcefully, they would treat him in exactly the same way. As he walked past the picketers, he spoke to them kindly and even spent a few minutes talking to some of them, suggesting that they come and listen to him sometime.

They might possibly see him in a different light.

Francis was already asleep when his hosts came home. He met one or two of them at breakfast, which he prepared for himself—a glass of orange juice, a bowl of dry cereal, and a cup of coffee.

"Sleep well last night?" one of the priests asked.

"Pretty well."

"Where do you go from here?"

"Back home. I came here special for your people." There was silence.

Then, after a long pause, "Well, have a good trip back," one of them said, as he left the table.

Francis found it difficult to understand their cold behavior. No offer of a gift or donation, not even a thank you. Was it resentment? Maybe they really did not want him there. Maybe they were just taken up with their own interests and had little interest in anything Francis had to say. Yet, if they cared, one would think they would be eager to hear something fresh and exciting about the person to whom they supposedly had dedicated their life. Francis left the place with an ache in his heart, and a sadness that stayed with him all the way home. It gave him comfort knowing the King had once been treated the same way many years ago by those who should have supported him. It was at times like this that he felt most alone. The unfelt but real presence of the King was becoming more than ever his only real joy.

While waiting for his connecting flight, a young man, "specially gifted," asked if he would like his shoes shined. Francis noticed everyone else had turned him down.

"Yes, I think I really need one. Do you spend your whole day here?" Francis asked him.

"Yes, most of the time. Sometimes it's discouraging. I support my mother who is old and my sister who is not well. Usually I do quite well, but I can't afford to get sick because then we don't eat."

Francis noticed the people sitting across the aisle were laughing quietly at the young man, as he had a speech defect. The fellow knew they were laughing at him, and Francis sensed he was used to it. He could understand how he must feel. Looking down at his shoes, Francis commented, "I have to admit, that is the best shine I ever had. You do a beautiful job. I can tell you take pride in your work."

CHAPTER

6

The next morning Francis decided to have scrambled eggs and herring roe for breakfast, something he was introduced to by a Baptist friend named Irvin. At the time, he did not have the slightest idea what he was eating, as his friend spoke "Southern" which was foreign to Francis' Northern ear, so he couldn't understand when his friend explained what it was. When he asked his friend's daughter afterward what her father served for breakfast, laughingly she translated what her father had said. It turned out to be herring roe. Francis enjoyed it so much he started cooking it for himself, once he found out where to obtain herring roe. His friend went fishing every morning and had no trouble finding his own supply of roe from the herring he caught. It is not as delicate as caviar, but not far removed from it either.

A phone call interrupted Francis' breakfast. "Francis, I know it's probably your breakfast time, but I had to talk to you. My name is Theresa McCann. Could I come and talk with you sometime today?"

Still recuperating from his trip, Francis was at first hesitant, but sensed an urgency in the woman's voice. "Could you tell me what it is about?"

"Yes, I am part of a large study group in a small diocese in the Midwest. I happened to be in your area and need to discuss with you an urgent problem. We are facing a crisis in our diocese. The diocese is having a meeting next week to discuss the problems we are having and I need to talk to you."

"Where are you now?"

"Not far away. I am staying at a hotel in the city."

"When will you be free?"

"At your convenience."

"How about one o'clock this afternoon?"

"That would be perfect. I will be done with meetings by then and will have the afternoon free."

Francis gave the woman directions to his home, then finished what was left of his breakfast.

Time at home was never restful. Phone calls were constant, the stream of visitors unending. After breakfast Francis spent time thinking about the King and how the King must view the kingdom. After his meditation he wandered out along the mountainside where he found serenity in the quiet of the forest. Singing birds and a whispering breeze sometimes offer more tranquility than a full night's sleep. The lady came on time. She was a woman in her forties, attractively dressed and, as one could easily see, a no-nonsense woman, a woman with a purpose. After the formalities, they went into the living room to continue their conversation, Francis carrying two cups of chocolate coffee which he had prepared.

"Francis, I appreciate your taking the time to see me today, especially on such short notice. What I have to share with you is important, and I did not know whom to talk to."

"I'm glad you called. Tell me what it is all about, and let's see if we can help in any way," Francis responded.

"The area where I live is an old part of the city. A good number of us are part of the old-time families who have lived there for generations. Over the years the neighborhood has changed. Many of the people are not well-educated and most of them not well-to-do. But they are good people. Most belong to the parish but are not active. The priests show little interest in them and as a result they are drifting. Outsiders have been coming into our area and show interest in the people and have been convincing some that the Church is not faithful to the Bible.

"They frighten them by convincing them that if they stay in the Church, evil will befall them, and they may lose their souls. Since many of these people are simple, they believe them. Many have already left the Church and are bringing others with them. Families are being torn apart. Longtime friendships have been destroyed; the whole neighborhood is suffering from what is certainly not the work of God. Peace, gentleness, harmony are the fruits of God's spirit."

"Have you discussed this with your bishop?"

"We tried, but it is almost impossible to get an appointment with him. His secretaries keep saying his schedule is full and he has no time to meet with us. We can't even get him to talk with us on the phone. It's as if he doesn't care, and would just as soon not know about the problem. People say he's a good man, but I guess he has his own priorities and concern for these people is not one of them."

"What can I do? This is a problem in many areas of the kingdom, and if the bishops themselves do not try to repair the damage being done, I don't know how I can help."

"Could you come and talk to the people? They trust you because they know you are honest, and are not afraid to admit the shortcomings of the Church, and will give them sound direction. They don't trust the bishops. They know they are political, and will never admit anything is wrong in the Church, when everyone knows there is a lot of hurt and injustice taking place all over."

"If you think it will help, I'd be glad to speak to them. Tell your bishop you had talked to me and that I would be glad to come and speak to the people. The bishop is an old friend and I think he will work with you."

"Francis, I can't thank you enough. I'll give the bishop your message as soon as I return home, and try to discuss some dates. Then I'll get back to you."

With important matters settled, they exchanged small talk until they'd finished their coffee.

As the lady got up to leave, Francis accompanied her to the door. She again thanked him and promised to call in a few days.

CHAPTER

7

Francis' first day home was not as restful as he had hoped. Besides Theresa, there were others scheduled to see him. The mail that day was heavy, much of it fan mail, some of it critical of the work he was doing. Affirmation from bishops would have been an encouragement, because he knew he was doing the work they did not have the courage to do, creating grassroots pressure they needed to negotiate with Vatican officials. He thought they would at least be appreciative. Some were, like a bishop in Texas, and others in Chicago, Colorado, and Virginia—and even Trenton and a few others. What hurt most, though, was information that came back to him. Indeed, from conversations with friends in strategic positions Francis knew he was more the object of ridicule on the part of many bishops, even those who knew him and should have been his defenders. Francis learned they could not be counted on when he was under attack. However, nothing seemed to dampen his happy spirits One would think he would feel a sense of loneliness and futility in the midst of all the opposition, and the seeming unconcern of bishops. Adding to his predicament was the painful realization that many good people could not understand why he was making such a fuss over the way things were done in the kingdom. After all, it had been that way for centuries. That's just the way it is. People who understood and appreciated his work were those who had a feeling for the King and were concerned about bishops not being faithful to the King's spirit. The many who were hurting, especially those hurt by teachers and clergy, also appreciated what Francis was trying to accomplish. Had he loved the Kingdom less he would just have left things the way they were. However, it was his driving passion to bring things into conformity with the King's dream of what the kingdom should be like. He had long since decided that if people thought him disloyal it would in no way influence him to change course, nor would he allow them to interfere in what he knew had to be done. Being sensitive, however, it troubled him that good people could not readily understand. When people were particularly offensive in their remarks, he would try to listen and see if there was any merit to their complaints. For the most part, though, he realized that it was his insistence on changing the way things had been done for centuries that was unhinging the security of those whose stability depended on things never changing. That explained why they could become so violent in opposing him, often accusing him of doing the work of the devil, and of laying minefields to destroy the innocent.

That night Francis' sleep was restless, broken by a dream which kept recurring all through the night. He was wandering through an imaginary village. The plant life and animal life were like what one would see in a fairy tale, with an illusion of unreality. The people seemed quite human in many respects, but there was something about them that gave the impression that they seemed detached from life around them. As he approached the village, a small group of people were huddled under a tree, sheltering themselves from the light. Picnic baskets nearby suggested they had gathered for a party. Everyone was wearing dark glasses. Each person was holding a book and reading it, but the light was not from the shining sun because the sunlight could not penetrate the dark foliage of the tree. Francis noticed a light coming from The Book itself, which illuminated the text sufficiently for reading. The bright world outside the shade of the tree, as brilliant as it was, they could not see; it was shut off from their sight.

As Francis walked past, he realized no one in the group even knew he was there. They just kept on reading and talking to one another, but the language they were speaking was not contemporary. They were speaking the language found in The Book. As they conversed, they occasionally smiled, but did not seem to be really happy. They seemed fearful, as if danger were imminent. They kept their children close to them as if protecting them from some evil lurking nearby. "How strange!" he thought. "Their whole world is focused on The Book, but they seem frightened of life around them, afraid of outside influences, and they associate only with their own as if afraid of being contaminated, which is so foreign to the mind of the King." Walking past, he overheard a father telling his children never to go near the village across the bridge because the people there were evil.

As he walked farther on, he came to another village. The people there were different. They also seemed to be observing a special day of some sort. A large group of villagers were gathered inside the walls of a cemetery. Though they were picnicking, they did not seem to be happy at all, but fearful, and distrustful, as if they could be easily hurt or broken by the world around them. They also kept their children very close to them to protect them. As Francis approached he noticed they were not talking to one another but each was wearing tiny earphones. They seemed engrossed in messages they were receiving from outside. As he walked through the crowd, again no one seemed to notice him, so he continued walking among them.

One man, obviously hard-of-hearing, had his speaker turned up high—high enough for Francis to hear. A voice was telling the people how they should think and what they were to believe, laying down strict rules for them to follow if they wanted to be accepted in the village. The voice further urged them never to socialize with people in the village across the stream. These others would surely contaminate their principles and the way of life for which their forefathers died.

Francis felt uneasy being near these people. They seemed not to be themselves but acted as if they had been programmed from outside, which made their actions and responses to one another artificial and predictable. They said and did what they were expected to say and do. They even wore clothes of a bygone era, as if they were afraid to become part of life in the present world, and were trying desperately to hang onto the things of a world long gone by. They were very attached to the law and the old tradition. They were the people of The Law.

Francis wondered how the good people in both these villages could be so different from one another. In their hearts they must have felt deep down that they were being faithful to the King, but their way was so far from the openness and freedom of the King and the spirit he wanted for his people. In being so closed and frightened of life around them they had become oddities to the ordinary people who wanted to learn more about the King but were afraid that if following the King meant becoming like those people, they could not do it. Francis found their strange behavior repulsive and offensive to one's dignity as a human. To Francis it was clear that these people were not free to live their own lives, but were being directed by others far away.

He reached the stream the people were talking about. The bridge crossing the stream was decorated with cheerfully colored designs. As he approached the bridge, he could hear happy music and laughter in the distance, as if people were just enjoying the beautiful sunny day. That had to be the evil place the other villagers shunned. Curious, Francis hurried his pace as he crossed the bridge, wondering what he would find on the other side.

As soon as he entered the village he knew it was a happy place. He felt relaxed. Surveying the surroundings, he could see no signs of the evil he had expected from what he had heard in the other villages. All he saw was a village filled with happy, carefree people who seemed to really enjoy the fun of being alive. Some were dancing near a gazebo housing a dance band. Others were playing volleyball. Some were swimming in a nearby lake; others were lying on the beach soaking in the sun. The children were running and dancing and playing games, and all seemed to know one another. No one seemed to be a stranger in the village. It was as if everyone belonged to one family, that they had all bonded with one another.

What struck Francis the most was the singular absence of fear in the village. "I have come to bring you peace, to set captives free, to lift the burdens from your heart," Francis could hear, as if the King were whispering into his ear. Yes, this is what it means. "I want people to know me as a friend. I created them for this. Their only law is the law that they care for one another and act out of what is good for each other and for the whole community near and far. They all belong to one another, whatever shade of color their outward beauty may assume. Each reflects what I really am, diverse aspects of my goodness. I am neither black nor white nor any in-between. I belong to all and am in all. Each can see herself or himself in me and know that I belong to them as well as to every other."

Unlike in the other villages, Francis was immediately noticed and welcomed. They asked him his name and where he was from. They in turn were free in telling him about themselves. Within only a few minutes he felt a part of the family, and was invited by a vibrant young lady to share in their celebration. She seemed to be the spirit behind all the activity. She would dance with children and give balloons to old folk, who were calling her "God's Gift." She radiated joy and innocence. He sensed she would one day work with him. It was clear these people really loved life. It was also clear they loved to eat. There were piles of meats and salads and vegetables and fruits and cakes of all sorts and they were certainly not for people on diets. It was all "happy" food. He wasted no time sampling everything. Of all the places Francis had been, it struck him that these people had the spirit the King had in mind when he founded the kingdom. It was a happy spirit. They were serious-minded people, and he could tell they were people successful in life, but they enjoyed life to the full, and were not afraid of life—no paranoia, no cynical suspicions. They welcomed life with open arms, with the simplicity of children. Everything about them radiated joy and serenity, which showed in the gentle way they treated one another.

The surprising thing about the village was that no one seemed to be in charge. It was well-organized, so someone had to be in charge, but no one acted officiously, so it was difficult to determine who set the tone for the community. Everyone just seemed willing to help one another.

An elderly man approached Francis. "Hello, young man," he said, "I notice you are new among us. Please feel at home. As you can tell, we are all friends here."

"Thank you, sir. My name is Francis. Your people have made me feel so much at home. I have never come across a people quite like you. Who are you? Are you all one family?"

"Well, I suppose you could say that. We all have different names and family trees, but you could say we are all one family, because we have become so close. There isn't anything we wouldn't do for each other."

"Do you have a name?"

"Not formally, but we like to call ourselves 'friends of the King.'"

"Do you have leaders?"

"Oh yes, but they do not call themselves leaders. They are one of us and place themselves at our service. They offer guidance and direction, but they respect us and the decisions we feel we have to make in good conscience. They do not make us feel guilty when we make decisions against their wishes. They are a friend to each one of us, and treat us as friends. We are blessed to have such leaders. They try to be faithful to Jesus' counsel to be servants of the servants of God—in reality, not just in title."

Francis was deeply touched. He could feel the Jesus spirit throughout the whole group. "If only everyone could live this way," Francis told the old man.

"Yes, it is so beautiful. I never knew Jesus before. I lived my whole life without him, until I met these people. They showed me another way and through them I met Jesus. He is now the sunshine in the twilight of my life. I long to see him soon."

Francis was moved to tears by the fragile beauty in the old man's manner. "I have never met a man with your openness and sensitivity," Francis said.

"Thank you, young man. It comes when fear leaves. I have nothing to hide, nothing to fear. I suppose it's the child's simplicity I have found in my old age. I guess that was what Jesus talked about, you know, the simplicity of a little child. Always feel at home with us, young man. Our hearts are open to everyone," the old man said as he walked away.

"Thank you, friend. You have been most welcoming. I am sure Jesus is pleased by the way you care for one another." As the man walked away Francis continued to survey the crowd. There was not a discordant note in the whole group. Francis was not only deeply impressed with the people; he was en-joying himself immensely. He had been eyeing a fruit-filled cake which everyone was eating. He walked over and picked up a piece and was about to bite into it, when suddenly a bell rang, and Francis woke up to turn off the alarm, distressed and disappointed that the party had come to such an abrupt end.

CHAPTER

8

The sun was just rising as Francis woke up. A cool breeze floated through the open window rustling papers on his desk. Walking to the window, he stretched and yawned with deep, sensuous pleasure and looked out across the meadow toward the sunrise. It was magnificent with its vast palette of colors and shades. He watched as it changed and thought of the King. He could always see the King in the sunrise and feel the comfort of his presence. Tears welled up in his eyes as he stood in awe and contemplation. It renewed his faith and his hope in the ultimate triumph of the King's goodness, as well as the fulfillment of his dream.

After breakfast, the endless stream of phone calls began. The first was from the other end of the country. The voice was apologetic and hesitant. "Francis, I hope I haven't disturbed your breakfast."

"Not at all. I just finished."

"My name is Thomas. I am seventy-six years old and am dying. I have terminal cancer. I am a priest—that is, I used to be—but my work helping poor people in the years after the Depression upset my bishop. When they made life too difficult for me, I left and married. Now that I am old and dying of cancer, I would like to make my peace with God and die a peaceful death. I asked my bishop in California if he would reinstate me, so I could offer Mass once more before I die. My wife is dead, so there doesn't seem to be a problem. The bishop seemed kind enough but said he did not know what the procedure was and said he would get back to me. After a few weeks, I called to remind him and he promised to call me. That was almost a month ago now, and I still have not heard from him. The doctor told me I have only a couple of weeks left to live, and I want so much to die in peace. Would I be imposing on you if I had a friend drive me to New York to make a retreat with you. You are a good priest, Francis, and everyone knows you are close to Jesus and you know his heart. If I could spend some time with you, I know you could bring me back into God's good grace. Would it be a terrible imposition if I came to visit you for a few days so you could help me?"

"But, you live so far away, and you are dying."

"I know, but it would mean so much to me."

"If it is that important to you, you are more than welcome,

but I don't like seeing you burdening yourself with such a stressful trip."

"It will be well worth it. I don't have much time, and I must make peace, not only with God, but with my mother and sister, a nun, who have not talked to me in almost fifty years."

"When would you like to come?" Francis asked.

"As soon as I can make travel arrangements. I have a little money. A friend offered to drive me. It will take about three days. Would that be all right?"

Francis was touched by the man's humility and by the frightful loneliness he could sense in his voice.

"Yes, of course. Are you sure there isn't someone closer to home who can help you?"

"No one, Francis. I am so grateful to you for accepting me. I will be there in a few days."

"I'll be expecting you. Take your time and be at peace. God understands your pain and, in spite of what you feel about yourself, you are close to God."

The rest of the day was quiet. In the afternoon, Francis walked up into the hills to distance himself from the telephones and find some peace and quiet.

When he came back to the house, a lady was waiting for him. "Hello, sir. Are you Francis?"

"Yes, I am. Can I help you?"

"I hope so. My name is Cusum. I am Hindu. I have listened to you speak and read your writings. I hope you could spare a few minutes to talk to me."

"Of course," Francis responded. "We can sit out here on the porch, where we are shaded from the hot sun. Do you drink tea?" Francis asked.

"I would love a cup of tea, if it is not too much trouble."

"It is no trouble at all."

As Francis went into the house to prepare the tea, the woman followed, commenting on the beauty of the surroundings, "This is a beautiful site, with the hills and the meadows."

"Yes, it is always so peaceful here, no matter what kind of weather we're having."

The front porch had a pleasant view of the trees and ponds and hills in the distance.

"I have been deeply affected by your ideas, Francis," the woman said. "In fact, I find myself being strongly drawn to the King you always talk about. However, being Hindu, I felt guilty about being so strongly attracted to only one God, since we are open to so many. I told my swami how I felt and asked him if I should be reading your books. I told him that many of my Hindu colleagues were reading them as well. He asked if I would let him read a copy. A short time later, we talked again and he said he wanted all his disciples to read your books and use them as their way of life. He also said he would like to meet you. He would like you to be his spiritual guide.

"Your writings have touched many of us in our profession. In fact, as psychologists and psychiatrists and counselors we use your writings frequently with our clients."

"I feel honored that they have meant so much to you and your friends. I never dreamed they would have the effect they have had on people," Francis replied.

"The reason I have come here is that I myself and some of my friends would like to follow the way of life your King proposes. How would we go about doing that?"

"It is very simple. What I have described in my books pretty well explains what is needed to follow the way of the King. It is important to make a commitment to him, because it is the commitment to him that gives life. His way is of value because it makes us one with him as a person, and we invite him into our life as a friend and guide. It is our acceptance of him and our friendship with him that opens for us a life that will one day lead us into his Kingdom of Light and Peace."

"I am prepared to make that commitment. I have found myself becoming deeply in love with the King."

"You are well on the way already."

"You mean it is that simple?" the woman asked him.

"Yes, it is that simple. His message is intended to set people free so they can live their lives in the joyful freedom that we were created to enjoy."

"Francis, I can't thank you enough for your help. May I come and visit again so I can learn more?"

"Of course you can. Just give me a call beforehand to make sure I am home, and we can set a time."

"Thank you."

As the woman left, Francis walked her to her car.

"I am most grateful for your taking the time to talk with me."

"I am honored you came. Thank you."

As the woman drove off, Francis stood and wondered, "So many followers of the King have left him hoping to find peace in the Orient, and now we see learned people from the Orient coming here because they have found peace in meeting Jesus and hearing his message."

Toward the end of the week, Francis' visitor arrived from across the country. He looked frail and embarrassed.

"Francis, I am so grateful to you for allowing me to intrude on your privacy and spend these few days with you."

"That is perfectly all right, Thomas. I just feel bad you had to come such a distance."

"It means a lot to me to talk with you."

After the formalities, Francis showed the man to his room. The guest asked if he could rest for a while before sharing with him his problems. It was almost supper time when the two finally sat down together over cocktails and snacks.

"You are not afraid of having a drink with your medication?" Francis asked, as he cracked the tray of ice cubes.

"Being so close to dying, I don't think a martini is going to make much difference. It's one of the few pleasures I can still enjoy," the man said as Francis handed him his drink.

"How was your marathon trip across the country?"

"It wasn't too bad, considering the short time we had to sightsee. But, I was very anxious to get here and spend time with you. There are so many things I have to discuss. In fact, my story is so long I don't know where to start."

"Just start from where you are now, and maybe go back as far as you need," Francis said.

"Francis, I have only a few weeks left, the doctor said, and I want to be at peace before I die. Since I left the priesthood in 1943, my sister and mother have not spoken to me for almost fifty years. I wish I could make my peace with them. I would give anything to say Mass with my mother."

"Why did you resign?"

"It was right after the Depression. Most of the people where I lived were out of work. Many had nothing to eat. I initiated programs to help the people get back on their feet. I was told that I should stick to the work I was assigned to do, and not get involved in those matters. I replied that I felt it was important that I be involved. I was severely reprimanded for not obeying and my life was made very difficult. When I felt I could not take the abuse any longer, I resigned. My life since has been very painful. Though I managed to accomplish many of my goals, I was never happy. I wanted to return to my original commitment, but was never allowed. Now that I am dying, I want more than anything else to be reinstated. I made this appeal to the bishop in my area. He promised to do what he could but I have not heard from him. I called him again. He said he was not sure of the procedure. Now, on the verge of despair, I came to ask your help."

"But, what can I do?"

"Perhaps you can tell me what I must do. I don't know."

"Thomas, don't you realize that the moment you turned your heart towards God and told him how you felt, you did all that was needed. The rest is formality. You know Jesus was never concerned about legal formalities. Their existence troubled him deeply while he was visiting our world. What was always important was what was in people's hearts. Your heart is right. You may feel bad about the turns your life has taken, but he understands the confusion and pain you have experienced in feeling alienated from him all those years, an alienation that was not even of your doing. During all that time God was never far from you, and though you thought you were alienated, he was still close to you. So, Thomas, you should feel at peace, especially now that you are trying so hard to do the right thing."

"But Francis, do you know what troubles me most? Not being permitted to say Mass in thanksgiving with my mother and sister. This has been forbidden to me since I resigned. This is what confused the bishop in my hometown, when I asked if I could be allowed to work again in what little time I have left and share in thanksgiving with the community. He told me he did not know how he could do it, even though I told him that whatever it would require of me, I would do it."

"What is important you have already done. You are at peace with God, and that is all that is necessary. Tomorrow morning we can offer Mass together, and thank God for his goodness."

"I may do that with you?"

"Yes, what is to stop you."

It may seem like a little thing to many, but the next morning when Francis and the old man sat on the porch overlooking the valley, that simple gesture of sharing in the breaking of bread in thanksgiving filled the old man's soul with a peace he had not felt in almost fifty years. He knew now he could die in peace. In that simple sacred moment there unfolded a thousand thoughts, joyful moments, painful memories, and hearts thankful to God whose acceptance and forgiveness knew no bounds, a gentle God who could pick up the pieces of a broken life and mend it in one quiet instant. The old man's face was wet with tears as they finished the simple ritual at a table on the porch overlooking a vast valley.

"You will never know what that did for me, Francis. It has been so long. If only I. . . ."

Before the man finished, Francis, knowing his thoughts, broke in, "Now, go home and do the same with your mother and sister."

"Do you think I could?"

"Why not?"

"If I could make peace with them, I could die happy."

The next few days went by fast. The old man looked tired, though at peace when he left. The companion who was driving had rested well. It was a long way to the old man's mother and sister's place in Minnesota. A week later Thomas called to tell Francis what had transpired. He celebrated Mass with his mother and made his peace with her. His sister, however, refused to come.

Not long afterward, when Francis had just returned home

from a meeting, he received a phone call telling him the old priest had died, at peace and with a smile, though he still had not heard from his bishop. The bishop, however, did attend his funeral and said many nice things about him, and the good he had done for so many people. The mourners thought it was gracious of the bishop to attend the funeral and deliver such a nice eulogy. Francis felt a sadness at the thought of the terrible loneliness, and hoped that not all bishops were as indecisive and pusillanimous as that one.

There was a similar situation in another city, where the archbishop reached out and welcomed back a priest in the same predicament, and, even defended his decision with the Vatican. It is sad that so many bishops are afraid to reach out and make bold decisions to help hurting priests. Perhaps they do not realize that they have the same authority as each of the apostles had to make decisions when it affects their own people, which includes their priests. Until the bishops together take hold of that authority, they will always be treated like underlings, only too happy to please their superiors.

CHAPTER

9

The best of the summer was over and autumn was setting in, the scenery around Francis' house was like a mountain on fire. Wild turkeys and deer, birds and little creatures of every description wandered freely around the grounds and near the ponds, feeling very much at home. They brought an added sense of peacefulness. Francis loved to watch them from the window. They wandered so freely and naturally as if it was their home. Later in the week Francis flew to Arizona to speak to a select group over a three-day period. A few were leaders, both men and women. One man in particular struck Francis' sense of humor. He was a plain-dressed man in his sixties, rather heavy-set and a little round in the front. He was wearing glasses and was slightly balding. His bright red suspenders and Levi's made Francis think he was probably a farmer. He sat on the far side of the room and no one made much of an effort to socialize with him.

On the second day, Francis approached him and asked his name and where he lived.

"My name is Richard, Richard Sinner. My mother's maiden name was 'Wild.' I live way up in North Dakota, near the border."

"That is a frightfully long way from Scottsdale, Arizona. Whatever brought you all the way down here?"

"One guess. Your retreat."

Francis was shocked that anyone would travel so far for something like that. "Well, I have to admit, I feel honored. Thank you for coming."

"I came so I could spend some time with you. I appreciate your work. You have been a big help to me."

"Did your family come with you?"

"I have no family. I am a priest."

"I love the way you dress. It sure is some disguise."

"I like to be casual. With the kind of work I do, it is best to be casual."

"What kind of work is that?"

"I travel to the Mexican border and pick up refugees and then I transport them to the Canadian border, where they are treated more humanely and can more easily find work. The government there is more kindly disposed to the plight of these people."

"How often do you do that?"

"At least every month."

"Don't you get arrested?"

"Constantly, but what can they do?"

"If the border guards know you, aren't they on the alert every time you show up?"

"Yes, but it is a waiting game. They know that I know that they have to leave for lunch. When they do, I pick up the people and take off."

"How do you finance your operation?"

"I have a quarter section of land that I continually lease out. No one uses it. They just pay me the monthly rent and with this I pay my expenses, and they have a tax write-off."

"When you get arrested, what do they do to you?"

"Not much. They confiscate my station wagon. But, who wants it. It's over ten years old. They end up giving it back, because they can't get rid of it. Then, there's usually a big headline in the paper the next day, 'Governor's Brother Arrested Again.' It's a little embarrassing, but, we both take it with a sense of humor. My brother is proud of the work I do. It's the way we were brought up, to help those in need."

"Richard, I admire your dedication and your selflessness. I imagine God must have many a laugh watching you perform."

"I hope so. I know I do."

"Don't you get angry with the authorities?"

"No, they have their job to do. I have mine. Even the ones who arrest me; they have become friends. You can't take life too seriously."

"You are amazing. More people should have your healthy attitude."

Richard was one of those happy, lighthearted people who

bring joy and humor wherever they go and in whatever circumstances they find themselves. Francis was overjoyed to
meet a priest with such spirit, a spirit that surely must make
Jesus feel good. He found out later that a book had been
written telling the life story of that remarkable man.

. . .

When Francis finished the retreat, he moved on to a place in
the heart of a big city. He was invited to speak at a center
where the homeless congregate. The priest in that area spent
his life working with these people. He had been working
among the poor and the homeless since his first assignment.
The homeless came from all around because they were
treated with such dignity and welcomed with such love. The
welcome Francis received there was touching. They were so
proud that someone of Francis' standing would come and
speak with them. They showed him all the things that were
happening in their little compound of buildings. There was a
clinic where doctors and nurses came on a daily basis to care
for the medical needs of the people free of charge. Down the
street was a restaurant run by "graduates" of the state peni-
tentiary. Francis enjoyed very much his lunch there. There
was also a drop-in center for the young people when they
came from school. They could congregate there and play bil-
liards and other games. Volunteers came every afternoon to
help them with their homework. The homeless people were
so proud of all the wonderful things that were happening in
their "home."

Francis' talk there was interrupted frequently by loud, encouraging expressions of approval. People had come from all over rich people, poor people, all kinds and shades, so well known and respected was this place. The music that was played, and which the people sang with such gusto, was the spontaneous manifestation of the joy that filled these simple people's hearts. When Francis finished his talk and left there, it was with a happy spirit and light heart. Unfortunately the whole program fell under a cloud over certain practices, which occasioned criticism even among good people.

CHAPTER
10

Francis' next journey was not enjoyable. It was the result of the visit from the lady who came to share the problem the people were having in their diocese. The woman had finally gone and talked to the bishop. He was not offended that the woman had talked to Francis, as they were classmates. He promised her he would invite Francis to speak to his people. Thus it came about. With Francis' reputation for integrity and fairness, the bishop thought he could help resolve the crisis. Perhaps he could also heal the many wounds that had been left unattended for too long a time and bring peace back to the community.

The bishop, whose name was John, met Francis at the airport and took him out to dinner, sharing with him all the problems he was facing with his people. Francis did not seem to be overly concerned and tried to reassure his friend that together they could resolve the problems.

"Francis, how did you learn to sense the mind of Jesus? At first when I heard what you were doing, I said to myself, 'God, he's presumptuous,' then I began to think about what you were saying and it seemed so real."

"It's nothing more than what we were taught in the monastery, how to pray, to contemplate. Being faithful to that, all the rest flows naturally."

"For you it may seem natural. When I make decisions, all I seem to do is antagonize people."

Francis listened as John spelled out the details of his predicament. After listening for almost an hour, Francis finally broke his silence. "John, you are a good man, and conscientious, but you focus all your energy on the observance of regulations and laws. People feel you are more concerned about rules than you are about *them* and how difficult their lives are.

"Your 'nice' people who pride themselves on being theologically correct, may be thrilled that you are that way. They are good people, but they are troubled by change. For the most part, they have had a good upbringing, and live disciplined lives. But not everyone has had the same background or experience. There are many others who have had disturbed and troubled lives. Many have been damaged from severe childhood experiences, or from inborn disabilities. This often makes it extremely difficult or impossible for them to live the way others expect them to. And they are offended when others demand that they conform to the rules.

They have to struggle harder than most just to get through an ordinary day, and they have neither the ability nor the strength to live in the way others find easy. To demand it and insist on the same rules in order to be acceptable in the Church is totally un-Christ-like. It makes them feel that they are not understood and that they are unwanted. That is why so many of them just walk away and never again darken the door of a church. This is why it is so important that our seminarians be taught about Jesus, so they can learn to think the way he thought and treat people the way he treated them. All they have been taught is how the Pharisees treated people. They punish people when they do not keep the law. Like them, we have become moral and doctrinal policemen, rather than the good shepherds Jesus talked about. When we realize that these troubled souls were the kind of people who followed Jesus everywhere, because he gave them hope, then we won't treat them so coldly."

"That sounds all well and good, Francis," John answered, "but I'm not made that way. I can easily identify with people who like to see things done right, the way things should be done. The others just have to learn to discipline themselves and live the way they are supposed to."

"John, don't you realize that that is what has caused your problem in the first place, not realizing that some people, with the best of effort, cannot measure up to what we expect of them? Put the righteous 'nice' people in the same environment and the same circumstances and they would be no different. People are just not that much different from one another. Some may be naturally stronger or tougher geneti-

THE MESSENGER   63

cally than others, which makes it easier for them to conform
to standards, but for the most part we are all pretty much the
same, and react from our own experiences and conditioning.
It is not that 'nice' people are good and the others are evil.
The struggle inside complex and troubled people to be good
is intensely more difficult than it is for people who are so-
called normal. In God's eyes, they are probably much more
lovable. To suggest to them that the 'nice' people are the role
models and that *they* are the black sheep is so offensive, you
can't blame them for being angry.

"John, if you really want to solve the problem, it is you who
have to make the adjustment. I know you have always been a
stickler for the right thing. You have been that way since we
were kids, and I am sure the reason you were made a bishop
is because the Vatican knew you were that way and could
trust you to uphold the way things have always been done. I
even used to admire you for your ability to be so disciplined,
but if you insist on this with these people, you are going to
lose them for good. You will be sending out the message that
the weak and the bruised and hurting sheep have no place in
your family. And that is just what is happening all over. Too
many modern Pharisees are sending that message out to the
people, and they are leaving in droves. How that attitude
must anger the Good Shepherd who tried so hard to convince
his Apostles not to be like the scribes and Pharisees."

"Is that all you have to say, Francis?" the bishop asked him,
disappointed that he was identifying him as the underlying
cause of the problem, and hinting he was like a Pharisee.

"John, I wish you wouldn't take it personally. I won't be

meeting with your people until tomorrow night. In the meantime, search your heart and look upon yourself as the mother of a big family with all kinds of children. How would you treat them, with all their differences and weaknesses?"

"Francis, I'm beginning to see another side of you. I never knew you to be a reformer. You were always so much fun, so carefree, when we were students."

"I guess I have just seen a lot, and I have not always been treated kindly because of the way I am. I think that must have made me aware of how others have to struggle to conform, and how difficult it must be for them. I have seen the most powerful examples of goodness in people who are troubled and crippled. On the surface they seemed undisciplined, and even loose, but once I got to know them I was struck by incidents of really heroic goodness and unselfishness. I will never forget this young boy I knew. He was not allowed to make his confirmation because he missed some of the religion classes. He was only sixteen. I saw him at the farmer's market selling fruits and vegetables at a big stand he had set up. Knowing he was not a farmer, I asked him what in the world he was doing at a market selling produce off a truck. I was surprised when he told me that he came across the farmer driving to market. 'The man had just parked his truck at a corner not too far from here. He must have had a heart attack or something. I drove him to the hospital, and after they admitted him, I told him I would take his truck to the market and sell everything for him. He was delighted. He trusted me because my father buys things from him all the time and he knew him.'

"When I asked him if he had trouble driving the truck, he

said, 'No, even though I didn't have a license, I learned how to drive my friend's father's truck.' Now there was a kid who was not acceptable to a very proper education director, but who in his personal life knew what Jesus was all about. Incidents like this have made me wonder over the years if religiously correct people, with all their allegiance to doctrine and law, are really as deeply spiritual or as Christ-like as the basically good and simple people who have problems with religion as they find it. Just because they are in love with the institution and what it stands for does not mean they love God, or have God's caring compassionate heart. Jesus accused the Pharisees of the same thing, of loving the law, but of having cold hearts devoid of love."

The bishop was deeply hurt by Francis' remarks, taking each statement personally because it fit him precisely. Francis did not intend it that way, but John knew it fit and it hurt.

"Francis, I think we had better end our conversation here. It is late and I need my sleep if I am to face those people tomorrow. I did enjoy the dinner, but I do feel a little hurt that you think I am partly to blame for the problems here."

"John, you know I have always had a high regard for you. I am just concerned that whatever wounds the people are experiencing might be healed. You have always been a kind man, and I know that you are capable of bringing peace to this community."

The bishop grunted, seemingly to show he accepted Francis' praise. The two men left the restaurant and drove back to the bishop's house, where Francis spent the night.

The next day Francis and the bishop spent hours planning the program for the evening. The bishop was really a sensitive man, though a very demanding administrator. He humbly accepted Francis' suggestions for resolving the issues his diocese was facing.

When the time came for the program to start, a huge crowd had already gathered. The affair had to be held at a large theatre-like auditorium to accommodate the vast crowd. Outside, picketers holding protest signs paraded up and down the street, accusing the bishop of being a turncoat and caving in to those who were trying to weaken the kingdom by being too willing to compromise. The bishop had tears in his eyes as he passed them. They had been his greatest support-ers as long as he did their bidding, now that he showed a will-ingness to heal wounds they turned against him.

Francis, however, was used to this, so it did not trouble him. In fact, he congratulated his friend on having arrived at a rarified stratum reserved for those who were not afraid to think for themselves. Many bishops followed the party line and in the process sold their souls as their sacrifice for polit-ical advancement, and all for a funny little hat. To be the ob-ject of those people's protest was really a mark of honor. Caught off guard by Francis' bluntness, the bishop laughed out loud, then caught himself, and resumed his dignified composure as the two walked into the auditorium.

When Francis was introduced, the audience broke out in loud applause. Though most had never seen him before, his reputation was well known, and people liked what they had heard.

The bishop was gracious in his introduction. "I feel I do not need to introduce our guest this evening. Though you have never met him, I can tell you already love him, so nothing I could say could enhance his place in your hearts. I do want to tell you that I am proud to have been a longtime friend of Francis', a friendship that goes back to our days in seminary. At the time I was very carefree and fun-loving. He was always meticulous and exact in everything he did. It was rare he ever made a mistake, and his reputation for attention to rules was impeccable. Oh, how we change!"

At which the whole audience chuckled, knowing the bishop was being facetious. At the end of the introduction, Francis rose to speak.

"My friends," he began. "Yes, our friendship does go way back. You may not believe it, but John was quite a cutup. He was serious, and meticulous, but also wild on occasion, when we were in the seminary. From what everybody tells me, I guess I was serious on occasion.

"Today, I am happy to be here with your bishop and all of you who have been so gracious to come. I wish, however, it had been under happier circumstances. Perhaps, by the time I leave we may have something wonderful to celebrate, and maybe, just maybe, we may see a shining sun and a clear blue sky. I have thought and prayed before coming here, and indeed, all the way here. The pain you are experiencing I feel in my heart. I just hope I can be of some help. Your bishop is a good man. He takes his responsibilities as a bishop seriously and does not compromise with the ideals he knows we should all follow. These ideals were sacred to the King when he was with us so long ago. Many other customs and practices have been added since, some of great value at the time they were instituted but of doubtful value in our times. When a bishop takes his role seriously, he tries not to pick and choose what is important and what is not important, but tries to be faithful in all matters.

"When I was a young priest, I gave up my carefree ways and tried to do everything as perfectly as I could. It was hard to understand why others could not do the same. It took me a long time to realize how smug I had become and self-righteous. I began to see that many others who may not have been as observant as I was had much more of Jesus' spirit in their hearts than I did. This struck me most dramatically one evening when I saw a fellow priest, for whom I had little regard, in chapel one night, deep in meditation. I found out that he did that every night. On another occasion I saw another person helping a poor blind beggar, gently guiding him down the street to a deli where he bought him supper. It wasn't just the supper that impressed me. It was the genuine love reflected in the way he talked with the man, as if he were an old friend he had not seen in years. Real goodness lies beneath the surface of many people's unpretentious exterior. Mechanical observance of laws and rituals is no real barometer of genuine holiness. It is only too often the veneer of a hollow shell, decorated like an Easter egg, with little inside but devotion to one's self-perfection. A person can keep the Commandments all his life and never do one good thing for another human being, because Commandments deal only with evil to be avoided, and not the good one should do. That is why Jesus could say of the Pharisees that they kept the Commandments but had no love of God nor mercy to ward others in their hearts.

"I once came across a lady who had been made to feel unwelcome in her church. Two elders ushered her out of her church service one Sunday morning because her husband had left her and divorced her. She was considered unworthy to be a member of her congregation. One day I came upon a scene downtown on a busy street. A woman had just spotted a child crossing the street as a truck came careening around the corner. Not having time to pull the boy out of danger, this woman ran into the street and knocked the boy to the ground. The two lay there motionless as the truck passed over them. When the truck passed they both got up unharmed. I then recognized her as the woman who had just recently been expelled from her congregation as an unworthy follower of Jesus. 'Greater love than this no one has than to lay down one's life for a friend.' Real goodness is often veiled in humility, and has no need of trumpets to announce its presence. I understand there are many good people here whose quiet, troubled lives do not fit into the neat format of others' expectations.

"I also know these same people have touched the lives of many by their goodness and compassion. That is the ultimate test of real worth in God's eyes. I know many of you here have suffered much at the hands and scathing tongues of those who judge themselves righteous and the models of Christian loyalty. I know they have judged you unworthy and unacceptable, yet you are the very ones the King would befriend if he were among us today. It is important that you feel at home in your family. No one has the right to exclude you or make you feel unworthy to participate in the life of the community or to share in the King's supper. There are also many here who have kept the law and all that has been asked of them. That is not an easy accomplishment. We can only admire them for their loyalty and dedication. This has value only if it is done with genuine humility and love, and never with a critical or condescending attitude toward those who do not have their ability, or the discipline, or God's grace to be that way. It must be remembered that others have gifts and abilities that they do not have. So many righteous ones of old kept the law and were found wanting in Jesus' judgment. No one of us is in a position to be judge of another's goodness, because none of us is without serious shortcomings. Even the best of us will limp all the way to The Kingdom of Light and Peace. So, we must all bear with one another, and learn to discover the goodness in each other. When the King was on earth, he showed a rare understanding of each one's differences and appreciation for each one's goodness. He could have found fault, but decided to find good instead, inspiring each to bring forth their best. We must do the same. This is the only way to bring peace back to your community.

"In finishing, I would like to assure you that if you are really sincere in following Jesus' wishes, by understanding and caring for one another, you will find acceptance of your own lives before his throne. 'With what measure you judge others, with that same measure you will be judged.' You will also be building a community second to none in its happy spirit and great accomplishments. Thank you."

When Francis finished, he received a long and warm applause. There were a few individuals sprinkled throughout the audience who did not applaud. The faces of those people were like stone. When the others stood up as they continued applauding, they remained seated.

When Francis sat down, the bishop rose to speak. The audience fell silent.

"My friends," he started in a soft, carefully modulated tone. "How my friend Francis has changed! I never saw in him what I just witnessed today. He was, I am sure, inspired to say what he did. I know, I was deeply moved. And I would like to respond to his plea for understanding. I am as much at fault as anyone for the pain and heartache our community has been experiencing. I now realize that, and I am truly sorry. I see all of you now in a much different light after listening to Francis' talk. From now on I want you all to know that I appreciate each one of you, with all of your gifts and talents, and, yes, even your shortcomings. I know you cannot all be like each other, nor be the ideal we all strive for, but I want you to know that I appreciate whatever good there is in each of you.

"There are not among you those who are worthy and those who are less worthy. You are just different, with different qualities of goodness, and different failings, like all of us. I want you to know that from now on I am here for everyone, not just for the few. In the future, I will take my own counsel as to the worth of those in my charge. While all will have the same standing in my eyes and the same concern in my heart, I will no longer accept nor look for the favor of the wealthy and the socially prominent, and those who look upon themselves as righteous, but will, if anything, show greater concern for those who most need our love and assistance.

"I know, in the past, I have had the reputation of attending parties and funerals of people known to be prominent and of means. This will no longer be true. If time and circumstances permit, I will in some way try, either by myself or through others, to show my concern for all in times of tragedy. Concerning priests in my charge, I admit I have used them to foster those things in which I and my staff were involved, while showing little concern for their work or for their unselfish efforts on the front lines in the parishes. You are the ones who labor unceasingly to be good shepherds to your flocks, often alone and with no visible support. I confess I am hardly aware of all the good things you do. In the future I will make it my business to spend more time with each of you, to learn of your work and assure you of my support, and even more—of my appreciation.

"I want to assure all of you that you are dear to me. It has not been easy for me to say all these things to you, but I say them from my heart. It will be difficult for me to change, but, I do know that this is the right way, and I shall not waver. There will be some, I know, who will not be happy with this. That is unfortunate and I cannot change that. They are still members of my flock and when they need me I will be there for them as well. If they choose to leave, I cannot prevent that. Even Jesus could not please some, and they were the ones who turned against him.

"In ending, I am grateful to all of you for taking time from your busy schedules to come here today. I am especially grateful to my dear friend, Francis, for making us aware of the heart and spirit of Jesus. I ask all of you for your prayers. Thank you."

Everyone was ecstatic hearing these words from their bishop. The applause was thunderous. They knew precisely what he was talking about. Knowing this, they realized he meant every word, and in one simple stroke healed the pain and hurt in many people's hearts that day. Tomorrow would be a new day.

Little was said between Francis and the bishop in the car on the way back to the house. John was very pensive. Francis congratulated him on his eloquence, and his courage. Once back at the house, they had supper, then stayed up far into the night sharing their concerns for the future of the Church. They never realized how much their friendship really meant until they found themselves in the midst of this crisis. That incident brought the best out of each of them. But, the bishop knew in his heart that Francis would pay a great price for what he had said that day, and it would not be slow in coming as his enemies renewed their attempts to destroy him by interpreting his messages as evil and insidious.

The next day, as the two friends parted, it was with tears in their eyes, as they both sensed it would be the last time they would see each other.

CHAPTER

11

Though Francis' talk was not long, the nature of the talk and the intensity of concentration it demanded drained him of every ounce of energy. Giving talks like that always took a heavy toll. On returning home, he rested for the next few days, doing routine things like answering letters and visiting with friends. He needed the rest because his next talk would bring him far down into the bayous of Louisiana. He had been there years before and had met a priest named André, who had been deprived of his parish because he decided to marry a beautiful Cajun woman named Juliette. It was difficult for him to find work after that, because his training did not prepare him for any other type of work. But apparently that was never a concern to most bishops, once a priest left. In some places bishops had even tried to make it difficult for them to find work. Such is their sense of justice and charity. It was at a time when André was out of work that Francis met him. André had always taken a keen interest in promoting Francis' ideas of freedom in the Church, so the two became good friends and spent time together whenever circumstances permitted. The first time Francis went to the bayous he was warmly welcomed and made to feel at home. The people there were earthy and real, just themselves, with no airs of self-importance or false pride.

For all these reasons, Francis was looking forward to his return visit. But before leaving, there were business details that had to be tended to, and a host of personal matters. It was also mushroom season and Francis had been looking forward to scouring the mountainside for oyster mushrooms and puffballs and bear's beard, the only kinds he felt comfortable picking in the wild, since so many varieties are poisonous.

The day before leaving, a priest from Australia by the name of Peter came to visit. He had called weeks before and asked if he and Barbara, his secretary, could stop by, if Francis was not too busy. Peter had started a remarkable ministry in Sydney, gathering people together as small communities of friends, just to be there for one another, to share each other's good times and bad times. Some critics faulted the program for not having Bible discussions when they gathered. His response was beautiful: "When Jesus gathered people together, he didn't then say to them, 'Okay, now we are going to study the Bible.' He gathered people together so he could teach them how they could care and share with one another."

Peter and Barbara arrived late in the morning and spent the day. Peter was a rather rough-hewn individual on the surface, like an American cowboy of a bygone era, but underneath, a gentle, sensitive man with a marvelous ability to feel people's pain.

"G'day, Mate!" was Peter's greeting as he gave Francis a bear hug that almost broke him in two.

"Welcome, Peter," Francis returned once he caught his breath. "And you, too, Barbara."

Barbara, Peter's secretary, was a pretty woman, gracious and efficient. Francis could tell, after only a few minutes, that she was an absolute necessity to Peter, as his quick mind and ability to make rapid decisions rarely allowed him to stay on the same planet for more than a few seconds. He was a dreamer and a gentle revolutionary, but depended on her to keep it all together and make things work.

"This is quite a spread y'all got here, Mate," Peter said, as he surveyed the place.

"Yes, it's adequate, considering all the visitors we have. Tell me about your work, Peter!" Francis said as they walked into the dining area of the kitchen.

"I try to bring people together and encourage them to share friendship with one another. Just friendship, that's all. So often today people feel that when they get together, they have to get The Book out and discuss it. I find that artificial and unnatural. Getting people to care for one another was what was important to Jesus, not to get them to read a book. They didn't have any book. I do get criticized for it, as not having any substance, but it is because people have lost the ability to appreciate the spiritual depth of what friendship really means. Jesus established communities which were like families. He tried to teach people to care for one another as brothers and sisters."

"I think that is beautiful, Peter," Francis said as he placed a platter of meats and cheeses on the table.

"Yes, and Barbara is the one who makes it click. She takes care of the nuts and bolts of the whole operation. I don't know what I would do without her help. You know, you really can't do much without women. They know how to put things together."

"How is the program moving?"

"At this point it is all across Australia, and still spreading. People share in each others' lives. When there is a tragedy, they are there to support the family. If someone loses a job, they do what they can to help with food and at times even with the mortgage. When a person's hurting, there's always someone there to comfort.

"And it is not just in times of tragedy. When someone is happy, they share the happiness. They also party and celebrate together. They have a wonderful, happy spirit that is contagious and is spreading all across the country. Don't you think that makes Jesus happy? It is loving one another as he loved us that really counts."

"You certainly have it all together, Peter. It is the way the Church was intended to function before it got caught up in power and authority, which was the one thing that seemed to worry Jesus. He knew it would destroy that simple, spontaneous community spirit."

"Mate, I'm glad I had a chance to come here and spend some time with you. I've been a fan of yours for a long while. You've been a great encouragement in my work. I'm grateful."

"It was nice of you to say that, Peter. I appreciate it," Francis said. "I just came back from a difficult situation and I needed to hear that."

"We all need encouragement."

Peter did not stay long as he and his secretary had to go to Pennsylvania to set up a program in a state prison. Barbara's family also lived in Pennsylvania. They still had a long trip ahead of them, and Francis thought it was kind of them to go so far out of their way to say hello. It was good to see a priest with such dedication and concern for people, and who had such healthy values. Francis had come across others like him, but he also knew that there were too many who used the Church for their own personal advancement.

The plane trip to Louisiana the next day was not long. André met him at the airport with loud cheers and open arms and, after having lunch at Po' Boys, the two drove out to the bayou, about an hour's ride. The bayous are like crooked fingers jutting out in all directions from the waters of the gulf. The Cajuns who live there are descendents of the Acadians who were driven out of Nova Scotia over two hundred years ago during a time of religious persecution. Most of them still speak French and their English has only a trace of an accent, but their colorful way of expressing themselves betrays an earthy passion for life.

As they approached the house, André and Francis met Juliette's married daughter, Monique, and her sister Rebecca. Monique had just come back from the creek with baskets full of crayfish. Though her hair was disheveled and her blouse, shorts, and bare feet were covered with mud from the waters of the creek, Francis could not help but notice the beauty of her simple, down-to-earth openness to life. Rebecca, just as pretty but a little shy, was helping her pull the baskets of crayfish off the back of the truck. Putting down a basket, Monique walked over and gave Francis a hug. "We were wondering when you would be coming to visit. André has done nothing but talk about you for months."

"I've been wanting to come, but it is not easy to juggle my schedule. Dead End is not the easiest place to get to, you know?"

André guffawed. "It's not Dead End. It's Cutoff."

"Same thing," Francis retorted.

While they talked, Juliette was in the kitchen preparing supper. You could smell it out on the front porch. The smell of Cajun food simmering is an experience one can never forget. It is so different from what you get in restaurants. Once you experience the real thing, you are irresistibly drawn back to the bayou to relive the experience.

Juliette finally emerged from the kitchen, drying her hands

on her apron, as she walked over to hug Francis. She was still pretty after a life of hard work and worrying about children. It was easy to see why André loved her so much.

"It's been too long a time since your last visit. We're glad you finally made it back."

"It's good to be back. You've become like family. What's cooking, Juliette? It smells delicious. I can't wait to taste it."

"Oh, just some roast pork and Cajun gravy. It's been simmering all day, that's why it smells up the whole house."

Seeing everyone so busy, André knew when it was time to retreat. "Francis, let's leave before they find jobs for us. How about taking a walk?"

"Good idea. You can fill me in on all that's happened since our last visit."

As they walked down the road, Francis' eye caught sight of Spanish moss hanging from the trees. "I'd love to have a load of that moss for my plants, especially the orchids. They would grow wonderfully in that stuff. Maybe I can take some with me."

"It's all over the place, as you can see. You're more than welcome. Take as much as you want."

Pulling handfuls of the straw-like material from the branches, Francis gathered it together and compressed it into a ball that could fit in his airline bag. "André, what's been happening down here lately?"

"Not much. The previous pastor was very old-fashioned and rigid. He was not much help to any of us, totally out of step with the people and life here. People would come to my house for meetings. We would discuss our families and what was taking place in our lives and encourage one another during family tragedies.

"The new priest is a good man. People like him a lot, but they are discouraged. They resent being treated like little children who can't think for themselves. What they have done here, and the same is true in other places, is pay lip service to the priests and bishops and then follow their own convictions. If the bishops don't wake up to what is happening, they will one day realize too late that they have become like leaders in a parade pompously marching down the street with no one following them. Oh, the people show respect when the bishop comes to town. They all say what a nice man he is, but he means nothing to them anymore, as they know he doesn't really care about the people. It is a rare leader who teaches anything of substance anyway. They may make a pious statement about two or three current issues but nothing with any depth about the concerns of the people and their everyday problems. So, the bishops wander around in their dreamworld of Church politics, and the people make the best of life on their own. What amazes me is their loyalty to the Church, even though the bishops show such little interest in them."

"Is it really that bad? I see a lot of things as I travel around, André. I know quite a few of the bishops are that way, and priests, too. And, it's the same in the other denominations as well. My heart goes out to the good ones who struggle to make up for the hurt the others cause. The good ones rarely get the credit they deserve, and they take a lot of abuse when they reach out and try to be compassionate."

"I know we are isolated here and don't get a chance to see progress that's happening in other places. But, I'm familiar with the people here. They are my people, and I know them. They have it hard out here. They are good, hardworking people. My son Jody and his friends built their own fishing trawler. It would have cost close to a half-million dollars if they had to buy it. They built it themselves, a beautiful piece of workmanship, handcrafted, better than anything they would have bought. They work hard, sometimes spending days and nights out in the gulf, trawling. He almost got killed one night when they ran into an abandoned, unlighted offshore rig far from land. The boat was smashed. The crew was fortunate to have survived, even though they were seriously hurt. Everyone lives the same way out here. The oil company that abandoned the place got off without having to pay a cent. Life is not easy and the people struggle hard for what little they earn. It hurts when the bishops don't show any concern for them. They can't help but feel abandoned. But, still they are loyal."

Francis said nothing. He knew it was true. He had seen it all too often as he traveled from place to place and saw how little interest bishops showed in their people. As he was trying so hard to heal wounds and reenforce people's loyalty, he just listened and kept all these things in his heart. Often when he tried to share his experiences with bishops or priests, they either did not believe him, or were annoyed that he would bring up such things. They were offended and did not want to hear them. Good leaders listened and knew his words were true. In their own way they tried to change things in the face of searing opposition from those who resented anyone daring to criticize the Church. They knew Francis' frustration and tried to encourage him to continue his efforts. André ordinarily avoided heavy talk, so once he unburdened himself to Francis, he changed the subject. For a Cajun, food is forever in the forefront of his consciousness. So that became the topic until they arrived back at the house.

Dinner in a Cajun home is not just eating. It is an adventure. That night was no different. Not only was the meal a banquet, but the fun and humor sparked everyone's good spirits. If some were in bad humor at the beginning of the meal, before long they were on the floor with laughter. After dinner, André's musician friends came over to play. In the bayous musical geniuses are common, but rarely become known nationally. These people are humble and are not used to advertising themselves. They are content to share their talents with their community and bring life and joy to their neighbors.

Francis' time in the bayou was brief. Staying with these good people renewed his own spirits and made him realize even more the importance of the work he was doing.

CHAPTER

12

From there, Francis traveled to El Salvador, where the Church had been established for centuries. He had been looking forward to this trip for a long time. He knew the people there had been loyal in spite of dire poverty and abuse. Wealthy landowners and aristocrats, all supposedly Christians, lived luxuriously in the midst of all this misery. They cared little for their struggling fellow Christians. Their love of wealth froze their hearts to the suffering and destitution of the poor members of their own parishes. Many of the bishops came from these wealthy families and allowed the situation to continue. This, unfortunately, was tacitly accepted, if not approved by Vatican officials. The impoverished masses so loyal to the Church were all but abandoned except by those occasional priests and nuns who were willing to risk their lives and favor with the wealthy and the powerful to better conditions for the poor.

The place he visited was the capital of the country. The bishop there had been a kind, conservative, traditional kind of priest, but once he became bishop and felt firsthand the poverty and hopelessness of his people, his life changed. He became the foremost champion of the poor. Other bishops considered him a traitor and spoke against him, thus exposing him to his enemies. Even the Vatican's ambassador to the country sided with the other bishops, letting his enemies know that he was fair target of military investigations and suspicion by the wealthy. Though these people belonged, in name, to the Church, they thought nothing of turning against leaders when their status and wealth were threatened. And any bishop or priest who showed compassion for the poor was a threat, because any help given to the poor had to come ultimately from the handful of the superrich who owned all the industry and land in the country.

Francis was warmly greeted by the bishop, a gracious man named Oscar. He was most grateful to Francis for coming, knowing that in doing so he was putting his own life in danger. Accompanying the bishop was a delegation of peasants who also were eager to express their welcome in the name of the community. They escorted him to the leader's residence, where a large group of peasants had gathered for a celebration to welcome their guest. Their poverty did not prevent them from celebrating and having fun.

The food was simple rice and beans and other local foods

which made up in taste for what they lacked in elegance. The peasants danced and sang and partied as if they had not a care in the world until almost sundown when they all left to return to their simple homes before dark. The bishop lived just as simply and shared what he had with the poor, helping in whatever ways he could to ease their lot. But every move he made and every contact he had was carefully monitored by spies loyal to the military. The military, trained at an elite school in Fort Benning, Georgia, were experts in antiterrorism and antisubversion tactics, which included torture and assassination. Their loyalties were with the rich landowners and their political cronies. Anyone helping the poor peasants was automatically branded a subversive and dangerous. The bishop was in this category.

At that time well-meaning evangelicals from the United States came to bring the Gospel into the country and rather than befriend the bishop, who belonged to the Church, they reached out to his enemies instead, since they had already turned against the Church. They also tried to draw peasants away from the bishop, which delighted the military officers, because it not only embarrassed the bishop, but made him even more vulnerable to his enemies.

That night Francis did not sleep. Whether it was the strange surroundings or the ominous sense of danger that almost smothered him. Toward dawn he fell into a deep sleep, but was soon startled by the crowing of roosters outside his window. After showering, he and Oscar shared Eucharist and breakfast.

Later, toward noon, people began to gather to hear Francis' talk. As the two men walked toward the large cathedral, they passed groups of soldiers lining the street and surrounding the church. The atmosphere was tense. After being introduced, Francis approached the podium and was greeted with applause. It was not only to show how much they appreciated his coming to visit them, but also to annoy the military, who were now standing with loaded machine guns at various positions throughout the church. With a translator at his side, Francis began his talk.

"My dear friends, I feel I have known you for a lifetime. You are all dear to me in a way you could not possibly understand. I travel from place to place trying to awaken in people's hearts an awareness of Jesus' life which most of his followers have long forgotten. You are different. You have stood firm in your commitment to your faith. You have been willing to suffer and die for Jesus, as many of your friends and family already have. So I do not have to tell you about him. He is here very much in your midst, not only through his powerful presence in your hearts and in each of your lives personally, but also very vividly in the person of your bishop, who, like the Good Shepherd, is willing to sacrifice his own life so that you may be free. His life is an inspiration to all of us. It is not easy to keep focused on what is true and beautiful these days. There is so much falsehood and propaganda even among well-intentioned people who are dividing the kingdom and sowing doubt and confusion among those who have been loyal. But remember, it is teachers Jesus gave you, teachers willing to sacrifice and die to preserve in your hearts the true message Jesus sacrificed his own life to impart to us. Be loyal to your bishop. Jesus is always at his side. Be loyal to your teachers. It is so important you stand together against all the forces of evil, hell-bent on tearing apart and destroying the Church.

"I know I will be leaving you in a short time, and I will go back to a safe haven with beautiful memories of you living in such anguish. I will take with me the memory of your great faith and allegiance to God in times of chaos and torture. You will be in my thoughts and my prayers daily. I also ask for your prayers, which, I know, are precious to God, because they come from hearts willing to give all for him. May God bless you all with courage and strength to withstand the forces of evil which surround you."

As Francis said those last words, he looked around at the soldiers glaring at him with hatred in their eyes. Francis and the bishop processed from the hall and were surrounded by the excited crowd that gathered outside. They were lavish in their expressions of gratitude for what Francis had said to them. Many of them invited Francis to visit their little communities which had been organized to keep their faith alive, especially if anything should happen to their bishop. He promised to visit as many as time would allow during his short stay.

Back at the bishop's home, the two men rested for a while and then went out to tour the city, where they were followed the whole time. The bishop had been advised on numerous occasions to have a bodyguard for protection. But he refused, saying that if his enemies intended to kill him, they would find a way. Bodyguards would not stop them.

"Whatever God wants, I am ready," he would say. "I am not afraid."

As Oscar explained the history behind all the ancient Spanish-style buildings, Francis was fascinated, not only by the manner in which his host brought to life a whole period of history about which Francis knew nothing from all his years in school and universities, but he was also impressed with the warmth and picturesque character of the architecture. As the two walked the streets, peasants passed by and warmly greeted them. Soldiers and police gave the bishop embarrassed, ashamed glances, half in respect, half in anger for having put them in such a compromising position. Their families were once his friends and he'd taught them as little children. Now he was the enemy.

Along the way they encountered a group of people of The Book. They guiltily looked the other way, knowing he knew they had sided with his enemies and in doing so made his situation more precarious. They also did not want anyone to know he was in any way their friend. Oscar smiled at them graciously, showing he had no bad feelings for them. Francis realized he was the real follower of the King. He lived The Book and everything in it that was sacred to Jesus.

After touring the city, Oscar brought Francis to visit a few of the peasant communities. The people had broken up into small "base communities" as they called them. These small groups would meet and share with one another readings from the Bible, and their insights into what it meant for them, especially in these difficult times. They could see so clearly how similar their own lives were to stories in the Bible about dying for your faith. Oscar had started these groups, knowing how difficult the times were and not knowing what the future might bring. To teach the people how to deepen their faith and carry on the struggle for freedom was critical. Being faithful to the King and avoiding violence was important. The base communities advocated peaceful means to attain their goal.

By the end of the day, both men were tired and went to bed early. The next few days were spent visiting other base communities. Francis was impressed with how knowledgeable these simple peasants were in their understanding of Jesus' message. He was also touched by the fervor of their dedication to God and to their faith.

Francis' stay in El Salvador was all too short. He felt at home among these simple peasants who were much wealthier, in their poverty and destitution, than the heartless landowners and their lackeys who greedily hoarded all the goods of the earth for themselves. If Jesus' parable be fulfilled, that kind may never see Jesus, except on the day he calls all creation to judgment.

At the airport, Francis said goodbye to Oscar and the small group who came to wish him well. It was with a heavy heart that he left these simple, saintly people, but it was a heart full of rich and inspiring memories. He felt renewed hope for the kingdom as long as there were leaders like Oscar and brave honest people like those peasants. They were the strength and backbone of the Church. With people like that, the kingdom had a future. A thought crossed his mind: Maybe the kingdom thrives best in times of poverty and persecution. So often the well-to-do, and the politically powerful use the Church as a cover for their evil, or to further their own personal schemes.

It was a long trip home. When he finally arrived and fell asleep, it was a restless sleep. His mind was haunted by nightmares. Unable to rest, he got out of bed, brewed a cup of coffee, and turned on the television to watch the news. What he saw was not the news but the continuation of his nightmares. He could not believe what he was seeing. His face was soaked with a cold sweat. His heart was pounding like a hammer. He turned on the lights to wake himself from what had to be an unhealthy sleep. But he was not asleep; he was wide awake. It was not a bad dream. It was stark, terrifying reality. The faithful, saintly bishop in El Salvador, whom he had left only hours before, had been assassinated. While the archbishop was celebrating Mass in the cathedral, and surrounded by parishioners, a band of soldiers had marched into the church and shot him in cold blood—young men whom he had known from childhood and who had served his Mass as altar boys. Standing off to the side of the soldiers, in the background, dressed in an American uniform, was a military advisor. It later came to light that the official who approved this murder and similar assassinations had only recently "turned toward the Lord and been born again."

CHAPTER

13

It took a long time for Francis to recover from the shock of his friend's death. He had never seen such naked evil before. He was fast learning that evil most often disguises itself in the appearance of goodness. His friend was martyred under the pretext of protecting the country from evil forces. What sick twist of logic could destroy an innocent man on the pretext of protecting people from evil!

But wasn't there a precedent for that 2000 years ago? Could those most like him expect less? But that is the paradox of human evil. Evil people cannot allow themselves to be seen as evil, either by others or by themselves. They masquerade as protectors of humanity. How many holy innocents are murdered for the "benefit of humanity!"

Francis tried to take time to be alone after hearing the

news, but it wasn't possible. The day after his arrival, a young priest named Andrew came to visit him. He was undergoing a crisis in his personal life and did not know whom to turn to. "Francis," the young man said to him as they settled down in the living room, "thank you for taking the time to meet with me. I have been going through a very difficult period in my life of late. I love my work, but I feel my life is a waste and I can't shake the horrible feeling that what I am doing is off the mark, misses the target."

"How do you mean that?" Francis asked.

"I feel that all my work has no real substantial value. I feel like a social club director. I have been conscientious in carrying out what I feel is my responsibility, and people are very involved in all my programs, but it finally struck me that it seems so meaningless. Our work is about keeping a business afloat, about programs, about raising money for ever more programs. I feel that all our resources are channeled back into the operation. We have lost our focus. I feel we have become like a big corporation that produces energy but has no pipelines to the outside world. All the energy generated is circulated back into the corporation. It is a closed circuit. Our self-serving projects don't reach out to others, to the big community around us. They seem to be all focused inward, and distract us from the real work of energizing and giving life to the world. However, I don't know just what that work should be and I am confused."

"I think you've hit upon a very critical point, Andrew. That is precisely what has happened to the Church. People have

centered whole lives around the Church and their little corner of the kingdom. They have forgotten that the Church is
only a vehicle."

"What should we be doing then?"

"The same work for which the Church was originally
founded. When it was founded, everything focused on Jesus
and all the wonderful gifts he came to bring us. As time went
on, the focus of Church leaders changed. As the Church became powerful and wealthy, and bishops were treated like
princes and popes like emperors, they no longer felt comfortable with a poor and humble Jesus. He was nudged aside
until he was all but forgotten and disappeared from people's
consciousness. Oh, we talk about him because it is the thing
to do and we sing his praises, but not too many people really
know him and he no longer has much effect on many people's lives. Andrew, you have just come to the realization of
what has happened. It is nothing to be afraid of. What has
happened to you is healthy. From now on your work as a
priest will be an adventure, because you are now free to
channel all your energy into enkindling in people's hearts a
renewed knowledge and love of Jesus, and to bring knowledge of him out into the larger community. You will never
again feel that your work is futile and without purpose. It will
be lonely and difficult, because many people, especially
bishops, would still rather focus on the institution and polit-
ical correctness than on Jesus. They will not take kindly to
what you are doing, because you will embarrass them, but
you will have the comfort of knowing that you are pleasing

God, by bringing his Son to life in people's hearts once more. He will bless you for it, and you will change countless lives through your preaching."

"I needed to hear that, Francis. Yes, that is what I was looking for without realizing it. It is so simple. And yes, I have the courage, I think, with God's help, to stand alone. I have enough confidence in myself to make my own decisions. They can transfer me and assign me to difficult and lonely places, but I can work there just as well as in busy cities. People there also need to know the Lord. From now on, I will glory in telling people about Jesus. It gives real meaning to my work as a priest. After all, what are we priests for, if not to bring Jesus' message to the world. What a joyful thought! Thanks, Francis. That's all I needed to hear. Now I can see the whole rest of my life so clearly. It is so simple. I won't take up any more of your time." Andrew rose and gave Francis a hug, and left without further ado, but with a renewed enthusiasm not only for his work, but for his life as well. Francis smiled as the young man drove off.

The rest of the day was quiet. In the afternoon he rested and read. After supper he watched the news on television. There was an item about the cardinal archbishop of Chicago. Although he was dying of cancer, he was concerned about the serious disagreements among bishops and theologians, among those who were more conservative, and those considered liberal. As a gesture of goodwill before he died, in an attempt to bring peace to the Church, he suggested they all get together and try to arrive at a meeting of minds that would bring a much needed harmony to the Church. He was not suggesting that they compromise on what was essential, but begin discussion. Perhaps, even clarifying definitions might be a big step toward showing they were more in harmony than they realized. In matters of law and custom, there is always room for discussion and change. Sometimes, change is not only permissible but necessary for the health of the Church.

Francis thought that was a remarkable suggestion and was shocked the next day when some bishops, cardinals too, who considered themselves great defenders of things as they are, viciously attacked their dying colleague. It was cowardly and pitiless, but they laid bare their real selves before the whole world. It was almost impossible to see how they could be sincere. It would, however, make them look good to others of their kind, especially in the Vatican. Still, how could they respect themselves?

CHAPTER
14

Before Francis left for his next speaking engagement, he was surprised by a news announcement
that the pope would be visiting the country within the next
few days and would be speaking to a huge crowd of followers in one of the western states. Francis was looking forward
to the event because he admired the pope for his great
courage and zeal in encouraging people to be more focused
on Jesus' life. Even though he was rigid in many ways (un-
derstandable considering the difficult circumstances under
which he struggled all his life in an environment hostile to
the Church), he was a good man.

Although Francis could not attend the affair, he returned
home from his next speaking engagement in time to watch
the event on television. The pope was a charismatic man of

extraordinary stamina, but his age was showing more than ever before. He had become so weak and feeble. Although he spoke little about the King, he encouraged the audience to become more aware of the King and to follow him coura- geously. He said that the world had fallen away from its for- mer ideals and if people were to regain the strong, healthy ideals of the past, they must be willing to sacrifice the illicit pleasures sapping the country's moral fiber. It was the only way if they were to be a strong people once again.

Francis watched the reaction on the faces of the audi- ence, especially the young people. They were spellbound, showing clearly that the young are inspired by ideals, even when presented by an old man. They want to live better lives, but where can they find the example they need, the role models on which to shape their lives?

The pope gave them that role model. They left the event not only inspired, but firmly committed to the new ideals which they had taken to their hearts. Francis was impressed. The great leader was an old man with rough, craggy features and a strong personality. He had kept his ideals, honed in the fire of persecution and lifelong hardship. While this made him unbending in his principles, and not apt to understand people weaker than he and of different experience, he was nonetheless a good man, still capable of inspiring the young, as he had so easily done in his years as a young priest and bishop. But Francis could see he did not have many days left. He was fast reaching the end of his long and heroic career.

Francis prayed for him that night, and for God to send

priests who were not just focused on law, but on understanding and compassion for the people. The words of Jesus kept
ringing in his ears: "It is mercy and compassion I desire, not
demands that break the people's backs and kill their spirits."

Francis thought about the pope for a long time after
watching him on television. He could feel the burden he was
carrying as he confronted so many problems and issues in so
many areas across the world. Francis knew the pope's personal life was centered around Jesus, and that he spent
hours in intimate communion with him. But he was also
aware that those closest to him were not loyal to him and,
now that he was growing weaker, were undermining his
Christ-like attempts to heal wounds in the Church, and
reach out to other religions and denominations, and, substi-
tuting their own unhealthy theological ideas, trying to make
people think they were the pope's. It is frightening to see
how they could be so devious in matters so sacred. Francis
could see the toll his work was taking on him physically, and
felt he could not hold up under it very much longer.

Still worrying about the pope, Francis took off for his next
talk. Actually it was a series of talks for nuns. Some of the
women had known Francis and admired him and the work
he was doing; others, influenced by rumors they had heard
about him, viewed him with suspicion. The talks he was to
give spanned a period of five days, during which he probed
deeper and deeper into the mind of the King and what was
important to him. By the last day of the talks, even the most
critical were moved by what he had said. They had never

heard anyone talk about Jesus the way Francis did. His love was infectious. They all walked away at the end with a renewed love in their hearts. As they were all teachers and professors, they would bring this newfound love with them into the classrooms and inspire thousands of students with a new understanding of God. That was Francis' strategy, not to look for short-term success, but to aim for the long-term goals, changing people's awareness, so that after a period of time a whole new generation, educated in the thinking of Jesus, could renew the world.

Francis enjoyed talking to the nuns, particularly. They were more open and more willing to listen and take his message seriously. They were also more gracious and appreciative. Rarely did priests come to his talks. Even when they allowed him to be invited, they still shunned his talks. "What can he teach us that we don't already know," was a common remark. But, the women were different, and they took his messages seriously and acted on them. The thought crossed Francis' mind so many times: How different the Church would be if women had a larger role in running it. Clergy in other denominations seemed hungry to hear someone come and talk to them about Jesus. Even though they belonged to other denominations and were well educated, they were always appreciative: "It is so difficult to find anyone who gives talks about Jesus. It is such a luxury when we find one." Francis never failed to be touched by the humility of these men, many of whom were more learned than himself.

CHAPTER

15

Just before leaving for his next talk, which was actually a retreat for priests at a college near Washington,
the president called and said the local archbishop phoned
him and told him he had to cancel the retreat. He had received complaints from a couple of bishops in the Midwest
who said they would take their seminarians out of their seminary if Francis was allowed to conduct a retreat there. It was
unfortunate, because priests, some of whom were theologians teaching in area universities, had already registered in-
tending it to be their annual retreat. Everyone involved was
shocked that a bishop would cancel a retreat for mature men,
professors at that. Francis sensed all along that this would
happen, but the president, who was one of his staunch sup-
porters, felt strongly about having a Jesus-oriented retreat

for priest-alumni of the college. Since it was for priests, and not for the students or seminarians, who could object?

Francis did not feel offended, nor was it the first time something like that had happened. It all turned out well, as Francis needed the time off to rest. Not long after that incident, while relaxing after supper one evening, Francis was stunned by the news that the pope had succumbed to his illness and died just a few hours before. He knew the man had become feeble and looked so frail during his last trip, but the news of his death was, nonetheless, a shock. Francis immediately breathed a prayer for him, knowing in his heart that he was probably already in heaven. He also offered a fervent prayer for the one who would succeed him, that he would be a kind and good shepherd, and a man of vision.

It was almost three weeks before the news broke that a new pope had been elected. He was a relatively young man, with a brave heart and a strong mind. He was also a scripture scholar, and highly intelligent. Francis had quietly prayed that he would be the one, and was delighted when it happened.

After his acceptance and installation, he did not wait long before making important though symbolic decisions. He invited Protestant and Orthodox leaders to come and work closely with him. That simple but dramatic act of humility created a whole new climate worldwide. Some people of The Law condemned his actions as a deplorable compromise of principles. They would have a very difficult time being loyal to a magisterium under his guidance, just as they disregarded the magisterium of the Second Vatican Council, as not being in accordance with their thinking. His boldness did, however, open the door to people of goodwill who were concerned about the future of the Church, and were looking for a chance to work for unity in Christianity. The new pope also apologized to all those who had been hurt and alienated by shepherds and teachers who lacked love and compassion for the weak and the troubled, and opened his heart to welcome them back home. He sent directives to bishops throughout the world to introduce courses in the seminaries on the life and spirituality of Jesus, so young priests could find their role model in the Good Shepherd, who showed caring and compassion for the bruised and hurting sheep.

It was not long after his election as pope that he held up to bishops of the whole world for their inspiration and example the martyred Archbishop Oscar Romero, who sacrificed his life for his people. As a truly good shepherd, he made the ultimate sacrifice to protect his sheep. That kind and saintly man, though snubbed previously, was finally vindicated, and honored.

The next thing the new pope did was to form a council of advisors who would share authority with him. This group was to be composed of bishops from around the world and would meet at scheduled times during the year and make decisions and set policy which would be executed by the permanent staff of the Vatican, no longer to be run by bishops and cardinals, which in the past issued decrees and prohibitions to bishops around the world, causing untold resentment be-

cause of their arrogant attitude. That one gesture on the part
of the pope won him the love and respect of bishops all over
the world, even of those who took exception to other changes
he had made.

Francis' life changed with the election of the new pope.
People of The Book were pleased with the new leader, and
many of their fears and reservations about bishops and popes
began to dissipate. Each passing day found new initiatives
undertaken which pleased people of The Book immensely.
Not only did he encourage people in the kingdom to take the
Bible to heart and use it to become familiar with Jesus' life.
He also pleaded with people of other denominations to respond to Jesus' prayer at the Last Supper for unity among his
disciples, and to work constantly for oneness in the kingdom,
so that one day there might be "one flock and one shepherd."

Now that barriers were dissolving, Francis' mission to
bring Jesus to life in the churches flourished. He was invited
to speak to groups who would never have thought of inviting
him before. Invitations came from all over the world. But
now that the fire had started to spread, the King no longer
needed Francis' work. Jesus was coming into focus throughout the Christian world. The fire was spreading even to the
non-Christian world. Books were being written about him,
people were talking about him again, and Jesus was again
coming alive in his Church. In the meantime, Francis' health
began to fail. About all he was able to do was write—of
course about the King, and his Father, and his Spirit working
in the hearts of his followers. What was happening was

nothing short of miraculous. The hostilities and suspicions of centuries evaporated like an early morning mist in the sun. A new day had dawned, and hope spread not only through out the Church but the world, as forgiveness became the healing oil that touched people's hearts everywhere, making Jesus' presence real in his faraway kingdom that had for so long forgotten him.

ABOUT THE AUTHOR

JOSEPH F. GIRZONE retired from the active priesthood in 1981 for health reasons and embarked on a successful career as a writer and international speaker. His best-selling books include *Joshua: The Homecoming, A Portrait of Jesus,* and *Never Alone: A Personal Way to God.* In 1995 he established the Joshua Foundation, an organization dedicated to making Jesus better known throughout the world. He lives in Altamont, New York.